War in the
1884 - 18

CW01455717

A Campaign Guide

The Gordon Relief Expedition 1884-1885
and
The Re-conquest of the Sudan 1895-1898

N.B.Wollen

By Stuart Asquith

PARTIZAN   PRESS

Published by Partizan Press 2007
816 - 818 London Road, Leigh-on-sea,
Essex, SS9 3NH
Ph/Fx: +44 (0) 1702 473986
Email: ask@caliverbooks.com
www.caliverbooks.com

First published in Great Britain in 2007 by
Partizan Press

Design & Production by Jay Forster
(www.generate.me.uk)

ISBN: 978-1-85818-539-2

Printing by J. H. Haynes & Co. Ltd, Sparkford

Front Page:
Baggara tribesman
(Artist: Bob Marrion © Bob Marrion 2007)

Previous Page:
Colonel Burnaby's gallant fight to the death at
Abu Klea

Back Page:
A Victorian print of British infantry facing a
Dervish charge during the 1st Sudan war.

PARTIZAN HISTORICAL TITLES:

1 The Origins and Development of Military Tartans
James D Scarlett

2 The Last Scots Army 1661-1714
Stuart Reid

3 The Armies and Uniforms of Marlborough's Wars Pt1
CS Grant

4 The Armies and Uniforms of Marlborough's Wars Pt2
CS Grant

5 Cossack Hurrah! - Russian Irregular Cavalry Organisation and
Uniforms During the Napoleonic Wars
Dr S Summerfield

6 The King's Ships - Henry VIII's Royal Navy
Jonathan Davies

7 Armies and Uniforms of the Seven Years War
- A Wargamers Guide: Volume 1 Prussia and Allies
James Woods

8 Cumberland's Army: The British Army at Culloden
Stuart Reid

PARTIZAN SPECIAL EDITION SERIES:

1 Sieges and Fortifications of the Civil Wars in Britain
Mike Osborne

2 Partizan Press Guide to Solo Wargaming
Stuart Asquith

PARTIZAN ARMY GUIDES SERIES:

1 The Organization of the Texan Army
Stuart Reid

PARTIZAN BATTLEDRESS SERIES:

1 The Heart and the Rose -
The Battle of Linlithgow Bridge 1526
Jonathan Cooper

PARTIZAN PRESTIGE FORMAT (hardback):

Always Ready: The Drill Halls of Britain's Volunteer Forces
Mike Osborne

Napoleon's Campaign in Egypt: A Guide for Wargamers
Charles Grant

PARTIZAN PRESS WARGAME RULES:

Forlorn Hope - ECW	Pete Berry & Ben Wilkins
To the Banners - Pike & shot era	Stephen Danes
Lace Wars - Horse and Musket era	Stephen Danes
British Grenadier - American War of Independence	'Eclaireur
General de Brigade - Napoleonic Wars	David Brown
Guns at Gettsburg - GdB ACW variant	David Brown
Bloody Picnic - 1901-1925	Dillon Browne
Battlegroup Panzer Grenadier - WW2	David Brown
Contact! - Post-WW2 to modern	'Big Sid'

CONTENTS

Introduction and Chronology   5

Part One: The Gordon Relief Expedition
 1   The Background to the Gordon Relief Expedition   7
 2   The British Army 1884-1885   11
 3   The Mahdist Forces 1884-1898   17
 4   The Gordon Relief Expedition 1884-1885   25
 5   The Expeditions Against Osman Digna 1884-1885   39

Part Two: The Re-conquest of the Sudan
 6   The Background to 1896-1898   51
 7   The British Army 1896-1898   52
 8   The Egyptian and Sudanese Forces 1896-1898   65
 9   The Re-conquest of the Sudan 1896-1898   68

Part Three: War Gaming the Conflicts
 10 Some War Gaming Considerations   90
 11 Two Actions as War Games   107
       El Teb 1884   107
       Abu Kru 1885   113
 12 In Closing   118

Dedication: This book is dedicated to Samuel Harry.

<u>Foreword</u>

There's something about Victorian colonial exploits that stirs the blood. Grim faced, khaki clad infantry faced by overwhelming numbers of tribesmen who know no fear and take on troops armed with modern rifles, artillery and machine guns while they themselves have only hand held weapons.

In the Sudan 1884-1898 it is all there - the 'fuzzy-wuzzies' of Kipling, the Indian, Egyptian and Sudanese troop types, the renowned Highland infantry, the 21st Lancers, the Camel Corps, the Naval Brigade, the Gatling gun, gun boats, arid terrain, the River Nile - marvellous stuff!

The aim of this book is to provide the reader and war gamer with some idea as to how the campaigns were fought and how they might be re-created on the table top.

My sincere thanks are due to Dave Ryan for his belief in me and to my long time friend Bob Marrion, without whose valuable input this book would never have been completed.

I must also pay tribute to my long suffering wife, who has provided unstinting support, refreshments at intervals and once again put up with her 'retired' husband spending hours in the study.

Stuart Asquith
Cobweb Cottage
Northleach
March 2007

Introduction

The purpose of this present book is to look at the Gordon Relief Expedition of 1884-1885 and the Re-conquest of the Sudan by the British 1896-1989 with the war gamer very much in mind. It must be stressed that it is certainly not intended as a detailed campaign history. The overall aim is to provide the war gamer with an overview of both campaigns, the terrain, the combatants and an idea of any other aspects which could be incorporated in a war game re-enactment of either conflict.

Chronology

The Gordon Relief Expedition 1884-1885

1822
- Egypt gains complete control of the Sudan.

1883
- Mahdist uprising; Mahdi Mohammed Ahmed of Dongola announced himself to be a prophet and led a Dervish uprising to set the Sudan in flames.
- Battle of El Obeid (3rd November).

1884
- Battle of El Teb (29th February).
- Battle of Tamai (13th March).
- British orders Egypt to evacuate Sudan. General Gordon is sent to Khartoum (capital of Sudan) to supervise.

1884-1885
- Siege of Khartoum.
- For nearly a year Gordon is besieged by rebels in Khartoum under the Mahdi.
- The British government, under domestic pressure to rescue the popular Gordon, mount the Gordon Relief Expedition.

1885
- The Battle of Abu Klea (17th January).
- The Battle of Abu Kru (19th January)
- Fall of Khartoum (26th January)
- Battle of Kirbekan (19th February).
- Battle of Hasheen (20th March).
- The death of the Mahdi (21st June).
- The Mahdi's successor, the Kalifa Abdullah establishes control throughout the Sudan.

1889
- Battle of Toski (3rd August).
- First defeat of the Dervishes by an Egyptian force.

The charge of the 21st Lancers at Omdurman.

The Re-conquest of the Sudan 1896-1898

1896
- Britain decides to re-occupy the Sudan.
- General Kitchener commands the Anglo-Egyptian forces and begins his campaign.
- Capture of Dongola (21st September 1896).

1897
- General Kitchener asks for re-enforcements of British troops.

1898
- The Battle of the Atbara River (8th April).
- The Battle of Omdurman (2nd September).
- The Sudan is re-occupied and Anglo-Egyptian influence and control re-established.

1899
- Britain and Egypt agree joint sovereignty of the Sudan.

The Background to the Gordon Relief Expedition

The peace enforced by the British Army of Occupation, left in Egypt after the 1882 Nile campaign, was destined not to last very long.

The Sudan, Egypt's southern province was, as a result of being invaded by fierce Arab tribes throughout its history, very much a country of disunited peoples. The Arabs, the dominant race over the more numerous native Sudanese occupied much of the country, particularly the northern and central regions.

Egypt had conquered the Sudan and by 1870 held most of the country under its rule. As within Egypt itself, the people of the Sudan suffered under a cruel and oppressive government that exploited the country's natural resources and turned a blind eye to the financially lucrative slave trade.

In an attempt to disguise Egyptian involvement in the slave trade, in 1874 the Khedive of Egypt appointed a British officer - Charles George Gordon, Royal Engineers - as the Governor of Sudan's equatorial province.

The son of a British general, Gordon was born on 28th January 28 1833, in Woolwich. After entering the Royal Engineers as a second lieutenant in 1852, Gordon served in the Crimean War and later surveyed the Turkish-Russian border. He returned to England in 1858. In 1860, during the Second Opium War, he was sent to China, where he participated in the seizure of Peking (now Beijing). During the Taiping Rebellion the emperor asked Gordon to lead an irregular army of peasants and adventurers. With this force, known as the Ever-Victorious Army, Gordon recaptured the rebel capital Nanking in 1864 and quashed the rebellion.

Between 1864 and 1874 Gordon carried out various diplomatic and military engineering missions in England and Europe. In 1874, with British government approval, he entered the service of Ismail Pasha, the Khedive of Egypt.

Gordon took his new role seriously and went through the province sweeping away oppression and establishing law and order. He mapped large areas, established trading posts as far as Uganda and suppressed the flourishing slave trade. In 1877 the Khedive appointed him governor of the entire Sudan and regions bordering on the Red Sea, a position he was to hold until 1879. Gordon introduced administrative reforms, attempted to institute peaceful relations between Egypt and Abyssinia, established communications and worked to exploit natural resources and further reduce the slave trade.

After five years in the Sudan, Gordon left the country, leaving a power vacuum in his wake. His appointed Egyptian successor was Raouf Pasha, who was neither by ability nor intent, a worthy replacement for the popular Gordon. Bribery and corruption once again flourished, but there was now an additional factor that had not been present prior to Gordon's arrival.

The Sudanese people had enjoyed a five year interlude from oppression and now, rather than accepting their lot, had seen what life could be like. As well as resenting the return of the old regime, the native population began to turn against the people responsible. The scene was set for civil unrest; all that was needed was the spark to ignite the flame of open rebellion.

Mohammed Ahmed Ibn Al-Sayid Abdullah was a Danaqla Arab from the Dongola province of northern Sudan and a teacher of the Islamic religion. In August 1881 he declared himself to be the long awaited Mahdi (the 'messiah' or 'proclaimed one') who would lead the oppressed people away from their drudgery in a holy war to a new life beyond. He was an austere and pious man who advocated self denial and virtuous poverty as counters to worldly sin.

Mohammed Ahmed's claim was based largely on the fact that he had the same name as the Prophet Mohammed, was the same age and whose parents' names also coincided with those of the Prophet.

Whatever the strength of the Mahdi's claim for the role, the people, particularly the poorer sections of the Arab community, were only too pleased to receive him. His self defined mission was to rid the Sudan of all aggressors and foreigners, to apply the same effort to Egypt and finally to install Islam as the religion throughout Africa.

News of the Mahdi spread like wild fire throughout the Sudan as more and more people rallied to his banner.

Small Egyptian outposts were attacked and, when an attempt to arrest the Mahdi failed, a larger Egyptian force was ambushed in killed in December 1881.

By the end of the following year, the fervour had spread northwards, almost reaching Khartoum, the capital of the Sudan.

By January 1883 the rebels were strong enough to besiege and force the surrender of the Egyptian garrison at El Obeid, the provincial capital of the Kordofan region to the south west of Khartoum.

The Mahdi set up headquarters in the town, his cause strengthened by the acquisition of numerous firearms and five artillery pieces, all with ammunition, as well as £100,000 in cash as a result of the surrender.

Cairo is over 1,000 miles away from Khartoum, but appeals for help had already been received by Khedive's government. Egypt was at a loss as to how to provide any assistance; the army of 1882 had been disbanded after the battle of Tel-el-Kebir and the subsequent fall of Cairo, and at this time the new army that was being trained by Major General Wood, its first *sirdar* or commander-in-chief, was not yet ready for action.

Apart from maintaining a small garrison at Suakin on the Red Sea coast, the British government took no interest in the affair, leaving Egypt to resolve the situation.

El Obeid, 5th November 1883
Following the British government's refusal to intervene in the Sudan and in desperation, 10,000 reluctant and poorly trained men of the former rebel army (7,000 regular cavalry, 500 untrained cavalry, 400 mounted Bashi-Bazouks, 100 armoured horsemen, four Krupp field guns, 10 mountain guns, 5,500 camels, 500 horses) were despatched to the south in the company of a handful of British officers, all under the nominal command of one Suliman Pasha.

One of the British officers was Colonel W Hicks, who having retired from the Bombay army, was a major general in the Egyptian service and who was now acting as chief of staff to Suliman Pasha.

The army reached Khartoum, where defences were being prepared, and here Colonel Hicks attempted to teach some rudiments of discipline and drill. He seems to enjoyed some success, as he managed to control the area between the Blue and the White Nile, immediately to the south of Khartoum. This resulted in Hicks being appointed commander-in-chief of the Sudan Field Force in place of Suliman and being tasked to retake El Obeid.

Setting out on 9th September 1883 Hicks led a motley collection of some 7,000 generally dispirited and disinterested Egyptian infantry re-enlisted from Arabi's defeated army, some irregular cavalry, 14 pieces of artillery, six machine guns and 2,000 camp followers.

For a month Hicks moved towards El Obeid, watched all the way by the Mahdi's scouts. Led by unreliable guides and without proper lines of communication, on 5th November 1883 Hick's force was trapped by the Mahdi's greatly superior force at Shaykan in the deserts of Kordofan and annihilated after three days' hard fighting. The forces of the Mahdi now dominated the southern Sudan.

One Uthman Ben Abu Bakr Digna, better known as Osman Digna was a Beja-Hadendowah slave trader operating in the Red Sea around the port of Suakin. He decided to throw in his lot with the Mahdi who appointed him Emir of Eastern Sudan. Summoning the wandering Beja tribesmen from the hills bordering the Red Sea, Digna laid siege to Sinkat, some 60 miles from Suakin.

The besiegers defeated both an Egyptian relief force on 6th November and a second attempt near Tamai on 2nd December. A few days later the force in Sinkat was destroyed attempting to fight their way out.

The Egyptian government now appointed Major General Valentine Baker, an English officer in the Turkish army and head of the Egyptian police to relieve Sinkat, but his ill assorted command of policemen and peasants was attacked near El Teb by Osman Digna's men and defeated.

The fate of Colonel Hicks and Major General Baker lost nothing in the telling, both in Khartoum and the Mahdi's camp. Suakin itself was occupied by the British, who considered the port to be important - a point not lost on fact on Digna. If Suakin was captured, the Suez Canal would come under threat and the Red Sea route from Egypt to the Sudan would be lost, as conversely would the escape route for folk still in Khartoum. This would leave the highly vulnerable River Nile as the only available route.

Khartoum was gripped by panic and work on its defences proceeded with renewed vigour.

Sir Evelyn Baring was the British Agent and Consul General in Cairo and it was he who sent the news of Hick's defeat to London. The British government, keen to reduce and ultimately withdraw the army from Egypt, did not wish to become involved. As a result, Sir Evelyn was advised that the Egyptians should relinquish the Sudan and withdraw their garrisons as quickly as possible.

Grudgingly the Egyptians agreed and nominated Zobeir Pasha to oversee the reluctant withdrawal of their troops and people from the Sudan. Zobeir's appointment did not sit well with the British, for he was a slave trader by profession. Feeling obliged to evacuate the Europeans from Khartoum; the British government recalled General Gordon, who was at that time in England, tasking him to make what he could of the situation and if necessary supervise the evacuation of Khartoum.

The square at Abu Klea.

The British Army 1884-1885

Before we began to examine the campaigns, some comments on the uniforms and weapons of the British forces in Egypt and the Sudan would be in order.

As a result of the 1881 Cardwell Reforms, British army infantry regiments were organised into two battalions. The theory was that the 1st battalion of a regiment served abroad while the 2nd battalion was deployed within the UK. The battalions were each composed of eight 120 man companies. A company was further divided into two half-companies, commanded by subalterns, each consisting of two sections under sergeants. Cavalry regiments were usually composed of four squadrons, each 160 strong. Each squadron had three or four troops, each of three or four sections, each of four two-man files.

The Infantry

The Gordon Relief Expedition was one of the first campaigns where an authorised tropical uniform was worn. The British infantry of 1884-1885 wore grey or 'karkee' (a Persian or Urdu word meaning 'dust coloured') uniforms, although the scarlet frock was still taken on campaign - the River Column of the Expedition wore them - mainly, it seems, to impress and overawe the native opposition. The first khaki uniforms were issued to 1/Dorsetshire Regiment in January 1884, and incurred the displeasure of Queen Victoria when the uniform was shown to her at Windsor. The original khaki colour varied from a drab grey through various shades of gold and ochre to pink.

The 1877 pattern six panel white cork sun helmet issued to all troops on foreign service was worn. The helmets were stained drab at the army clothing factory in Pimlico before being issued to the troops. The chin chain was made from interlocking brass rings on a white leather backing. Issued with the helmet were an anti-insect curtain of fine green netting and goggles with smoked lenses to combat the glare of the sun.

The infantry were equipped with a reduced version of the 1871 or 1873 valise pattern equipment in buff leather. The valise itself was not carried; it rarely was on active service. An extra ammunition pouch of black leather was often hung from the rear of the brown or white leather waistbelt. The issue 1875 wooden Oliver pattern water bottle was carried on a strap over the left shoulder, the white linen haversack or ration bag was on the left hip with a strap over the right shoulder. Rifle slings were white or stained. Officers' pistol holsters were brown leather.

The standard British infantry weapon was the .45 inch calibre breech loading Martini-Henry Mark III rifle, first issued in 1874. Destined to be the last general issue weapon to use black powder, the rifle was a single shot weapon with a very simple action and an effective range of about 800 yards, although it was sighted for 1,450 yards. The weapon had a maximum rate of fire of 23 unaimed shots per minute, but 8-12 aimed rounds was a more likely figure in action. The rifle weighed 8lbs 10ozs and had a barrel 33 inches long.

Officers wore the Sam Browne belt with sword and pistol. Their official weapon was the .476 inch calibre MkII Enfield, but many privately purchased weapons were carried.

The Indian infantry were armed with the .577 calibre 1867 Snider-Enfield rifle.

Each man carried 70 rounds of ammunition and infantry battalions were issued with 28,800 rounds. The infantry ammunition column consisted of 43 small arms ammunition carts with 364,000 cartridges

The men carried one day's rations. Two day's rations, their greatcoats, plus 2lbs of fuel per man were moved with the regimental carts. Five days' rations, plus further fuel followed by train.

The infantry and indeed all other army personnel were issued with blue fisherman's sweaters when reaching Egypt. These were designed to wear at night to counter the freezing desert temperatures.

Mounted Infantry

In addition to their normal infantry equipment, the men of the mounted infantry companies were issued with Martini-Henry rifles and sword bayonets, plus a leather bandolier containing 100 rounds of ammunition which was worn over the shoulder.

The Cavalry

All ranks of the hussars wore the blue frock with shoulder chains.

The waist belts were of brown leather. The cavalry carried the Martini-Henry carbine and the sword.

The cavalry contingents of the Gordon Relief Expedition were mounted on small horses taken over from Egyptian cavalry units.

The Camel Corps

The Camel Corps raised in England for the Gordon Relief Expedition consisted of four regiments.

The Guards Camel Regiment under Colonel the Honourable Edward Boscawen, Coldstream Guards, consisted of four companies, each formed from 43 rank and file, including two NCOs and a bugler, taken from each of the three battalions of the Grenadier Guards, the 1st and 2nd Battalions of the Coldstream Guards and the 1st and 2nd Battalions the Scots Guards. The Royal Marine Camel Regiment was bracketed with that of the Guards and consisted of three officers and 102 NCOs and men of the Royal Marine Light Infantry under Major W H Poe.

The Heavy Cavalry Camel Regiment (Colonel the Honourable R Talbot, 1st Life Guards commanding) consisted of two officers and 43 men (including a trumpeter) taken from the 1st Life Guards, 2nd Life Guards, Royal Horse Guards, 2nd Dragoon Guards, 4th Dragoon Guards, 5th Dragoon Guards, 1st (Royal) Dragoons, 2nd Dragoons (Scots Greys), 5th Lancers and 16th Lancers.

The Light Camel Regiment (Colonel Stanley Clarke) was formed from contingents of two officers and 43 other ranks from the 3rd, 4th, 7th, 11th, 15th, 18th, 20th and 21st Hussars.

The Mounted Infantry Camel Regiment under Major the Honourable George Gough was organised into four companies; 'A', 'B', 'C' and 'D'.

'A', 'B' and 'D' companies had one officer and 30 other ranks drawn from various infantry battalions as follows:

'A' Company 1/South Staffordshire, 1/Gordon Highlanders, 1/The Black Watch (Royal Highlanders) and 3/King's Royal Rifle Corps.

'B' Company 1/The Queen's Own (Royal West Kent), 1/Royal Sussex, 2/Essex, 2/Duke of Cornwall's Light Infantry.

Soldiers of the camel borne infantry being introduced to their mounts. Note the saddles.
(Illustrated London News)

'D' Company 1/Prince Albert's (Somerset Light Infantry), 2/The Queen's Own (Royal West Kent), 2/Connaught Rangers, 1/Royal Scots (Lothian Regiment).

'C' Company was drawn from two battalions, each providing two officers and 60 other ranks; 3/King's Royal Rifle Corps, 2/Rifle Brigade.

The personnel of the Camel Corps wore a newly introduced grey foreign service uniform. The shade of grey serge worn is difficult to determine, but appears to have been a medium blue-grey when issued for other ranks, but this would have faded with service. The frock had a small standing collar and was single breasted, fastening with five brass buttons. There were no pockets on the breast or skirts, but there was a strap on each shoulder fastened by a small brass button. Rank chevrons were usually red although sometimes gold chevrons were in evidence. The majority of the officers sported a custom made jacket in a lighter grey, based on the style of the cavalry fatigue jacket.

Breeches for all ranks were made from Bedford cord and were a warm stone colour, reinforced on the insides of the leg. The rank and file wore dark blue puttees with brown ankle boots without spurs, the officers wore brown leather boots, puttees or canvas gaiters with ankle boots and favoured wearing spurs.

The other ranks of the Heavy Camel Regiment cut out numerals and letters from old red serge frocks and sewed their regimental designations on the upper right arm near the shoulder - '5L' for the 5th Lancers etc., while the men of the Mounted Infantry Camel Regiment stitched the shoulder straps from their old frocks to the sides of their helmets, while their officers wore the centres of their full dress helmet plate as badges.

A brown leather cartridge bandolier holding 50 rounds of ammunition was worn over the left shoulder, with a white linen haversack and a wooden 'Oliver' pattern water bottle carried on a white strap over the right shoulder. A brown leather waist belt was worn with an extra buff leather cartridge pouch from the valise pattern infantry equipment was carried on the right hand side.

The Camel Regiment parading prior to their embarkation to the Sudan.
(Illustrated London News)

The Royal Artillery

In late July 1884 the artillery battery accompanying the Desert Column was commanded by Captain Norton. The battery was equipped with three 7pdr rifled muzzle loading guns normally used by mountain batteries. On 5th September the unit exchanged their mules for camels. The three guns required the services of 42 camels, including three gun camels, three carriage camels, three wheel camels, three spare gun cradle camels, three spare carriage camels, three spare wheel camels and 15 ammunition camels. The officers, NCOs and trumpeters rode riding camels and the gunners rode the baggage camels along with their guns. Coming into action, the camel carrying the carriage was made to kneel first and the carriage lifted clear and placed three yards away. The barrel was not lifted until the carriage was set and its camel moved on.

The Royal Artillery wore a white helmet, dark blue tunic and trousers. The tunic collar was red, with yellow trim applied to the bottom edge. The blue shoulder straps were piped yellow and the ornate cuff lace was also yellow. The trousers had a narrow red stripe down the outer seam. The equipment and helmet were white.

Royal Engineer Uniforms

White helmet and cloth. Red frocks with dark blue collar and cuffs, the latter with yellow piping. Dark blue trousers with two red stripes on the outer seam, brown calf length gaiters.

Royal Marine Uniforms

The Royal Marine Light Infantry seem to have worn their undress blue uniform in the Sudan, as opposed to their full dress scarlet tunics with dark blue collar and cuffs. The usual white helmet was worn and the blue uniform was relieved only by a narrow red trouser seam. The equipment was either black or white leather, or a mix of both. The Royal Marine Artillery also wore a dark blue uniform. The tunic collar was red, with a yellow trim applied to the bottom edge. The blue shoulder straps were piped yellow and the cuff lace was also yellow. The narrow trouser seam was red. The equipment and helmet were white.

The Naval Brigade

There was great variance in the uniforms worn by the Naval Brigade. The seamen of a landing party might wear a straw coloured, wide brimmed, Sennet hat, a dark blue serge blouse over a white vest, white trousers, canvas leggings, black equipment and boots. A blanket roll could be carried over the right shoulder; the water bottles were covered in grey felt.

Black leather equipment, and a Martini-Henry rifle with a special cutlass/bayonet that could be used either on the rifle or as a sword was carried.

Regulation dress for officers in hot climates was a white helmet with a blue *pagri* or a white one edged with a blue line along the top edge. They also wore a single breasted white drill jacket with a low standing collar. The jacket fastened with five gilt buttons. Rank insignia was carried on the cuffs in either white silk or gold braid. White trousers and shoes completed the uniform. In fact double breasted dark blue reefer jackets were worn or a single breasted garment similar to the army frock in plan dark blue. The collar was worn turned down to show a white shirt and black tie. Headdress varied considerably and riding breeches or white duck trousers were worn with high boots, leggings or canvas gaiters.

The 1st Division of the Naval Brigade served with the Desert Column. Commanded by the Naval Attache,

A driver of the Army Service Corps wearing Service Dress c1898.

A type of hot weather uniform worn by naval officers in the Sudan. Variations may have occurred in the nether wear, trousers often being replaced by breeches of cavalry twill etc.

Captain Lord Charles Beresford RN, it comprised four officers and 53 NCOs and ratings. Parties of 'blue jackets' were also at Kirkeban with the River Column.

The .450 calibre Gardner gun used by the Naval Brigade was mounted on a 7lb field gun carriage fitted with a special mounting to enable the weapon to fire though a 180 degree arc. The gun had five barrels in a brass casing and fired just under 400 rounds per minute.

The Boatmen

Lord Wolseley had requested 400 Canadian 'shantymen' or 'voyageurs' to work with the West African 'kroomen' to handle the 32 feet long whaling boats that would journey up the River Nile.

The French Canadians formed the major part of this group, although there were also 'English' Canadians as well as some Canadian Indians. The whole unit was commanded by Captain Denison of the South Staffords, assisted by a staff of six officers and 18 civilian overseers. Although an unarmed civilian organisation, the boatmen were issued with helmets, dark grey Norfolk jackets and trousers, along with hard wearing moccasins, a blue flannel shirt and, as an alternative head dress, a soft grey felt hat. Their personal belongings were carried in a canvas haversack. The officers were the standard campaign dress.

The Mahdist Forces 1884-1898

The Mahdi and his disciples managed to unite most of the nomadic and pastoral peoples who lived in the vast arid lands to the south and west of upper Egypt. The peoples of the Sudan are basically Hamitic Arabs in the north and negroes in the south. The Arabs are sub-divided into several major races, the Ababdeha in the north, the Beja around the port of Suakin, the Bisharin south of Wadi Halfa and to the north of Debba, as well as the Kababish, Hassaniyeh and Shaguyeh around Khartoum. South of that city are the Baggara, with the Amara near Abu Hamed.

Each of these major races was further sub-divided into a number of tribes. For example the Beja contained the Hadendowah and the Taaisha.

Other tribes mentioned in various accounts include the Allanga, Barabra, Base, Batahin, Berberin, Dongala or Danaqla, Duguaim, Hamr-Kordofan, Hau-hau-hin, Jaalin or Ja'aliyin, Kenana, Monassir, Robatab, Shukreeyeh and Sowarab.

Early in his career, the Mahdi referred to his followers as Dervishes, which translates as 'poor men', but he changed this to refer to them as Ansar or 'followers' - those who consecrate themselves to God in the hope of paradise to come.

The Mahdi's forces were always referred to as 'Dervishes' by the British - probably seen as a corruption of the Persian word 'darvish' which originally meant 'beggar'.

Organisation

From 1885 the Mahdist army was effectively led by Khalifa Abdullahi. Arguably the most effective field commander was Osman Digna, who became senior Emir on the death of Abd al Rahman Mujumi and remained well placed in the hierarchy until Omdurman 1898.

The Dervish commander at Atbara was Khalifa Sharif Mahmud Ahmad, who was captured.

The Mahdi divided his main army of Dervishes into three main sections or corps based in Omdurman. Each of these was known as a *'rayya'* or 'Flag' and was commanded by a *khalifa* (apostle) who had a distinctively coloured flag. The Khalifa Abdullahi appointed his

Populating the northern part of the Sudan were the Hamitic Arabs. Forming the backbone of the Dervish army, they proved formidable and fanatical opponents.

A contemporary illustration showing various types of Arabs inhabiting the Sudan.

half-brother Yaqub to command the Black Flag and his eldest son Shaikh Uthman al-Din to command the Dark Green Flag. The (bright) Green Flag was a residual unit that had absorbed the Red Flag of Khgalifa al-Sharif; poorly armed it was recruited on a tribal basis in the White Nile area, from the more settled tribes.

Units guarding the *khalifas* were termed '*mulazamin*' and their numbers were drawn from the sons of noted tribal leaders. Such formations had elite status and were the best of the ansars.

The natives within the three Flags were further divided into units or 'rubs' (literally 'quarters') of between 800-1,200 men. These were further divided into three fighting formations plus an administrative section. The first unit was composed of spearmen, sub-divided into 'standards' made up of tribes or sections of tribes, then came the *jihadiyya* who were armed with rifles. Finally, the cavalry unit armed with long spears or rifles when on specific missions. Each 'standard' was further sub-divided into 'hundreds'.

Generally, just one tribe or a combination of two sub-tribes would make up such a unit and would be led by a mounted and splendidly dressed leader. Further sub-divisions of 100 men within these units would be commanded by local sheiks, while smaller sections of perhaps 25 were led by local sheiks; '*maggudamen*' or '*muqaddam*'.

A separate unit, entitled the '*Jehadia*' or '*Jihadiyya*' - 'the children of the holy war' - was formed from southern Sudanese who had been in the Egyptian army. Commanded by Hamdan Abu Anja, these men were armed with rifles and organised as an independent force that could be distributed amongst the Flags as required.

Outside this organisation were spearmen and swordsmen in tribal levy units, organised into separate commands in differing provinces.

The cavalry usually came from the horse owning Baggara (or Baqqara) tribesmen.

Appearance

There are two schools of thought regarding the appearance of the emirs (amirs) or leaders. One opinion is that they would dress in high conical helmets with finials topped

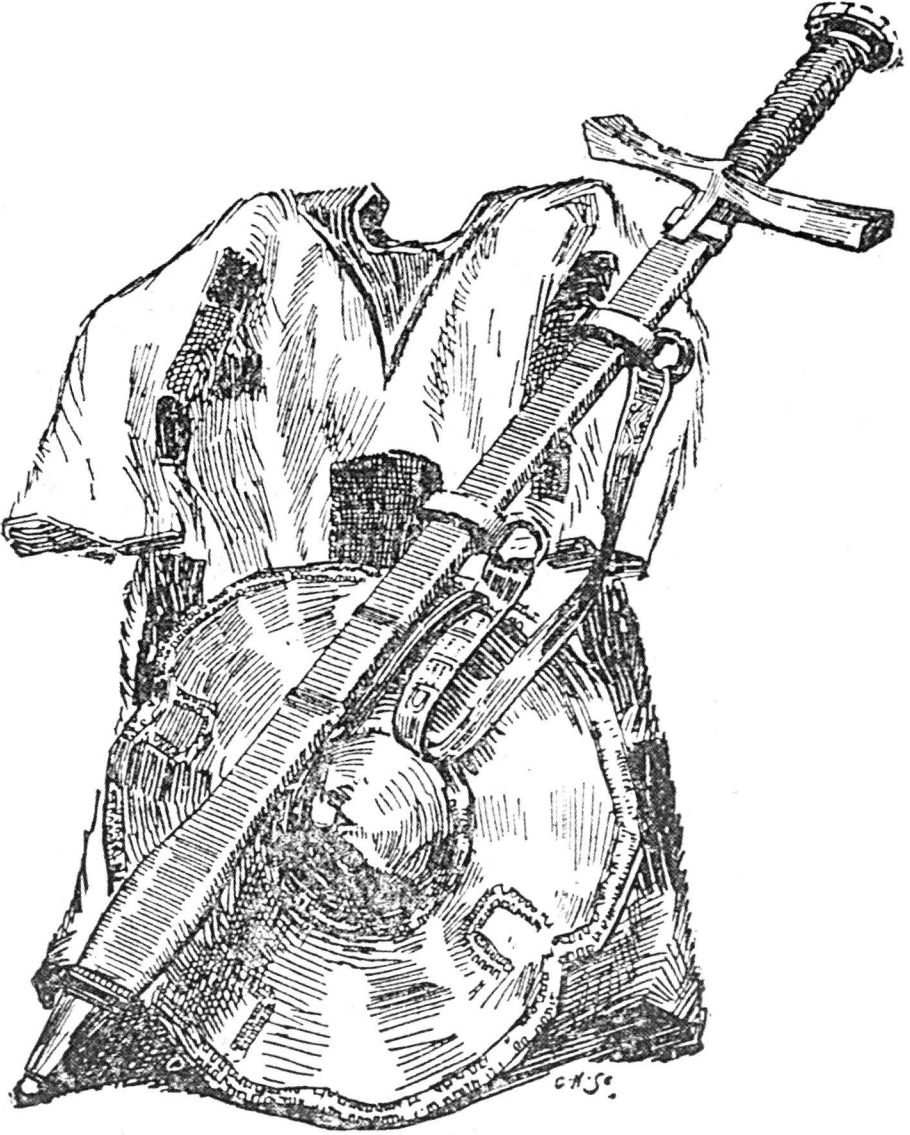

Typical Dervish equipment.

The Hadendowah tribesmen or 'Fuzzy-Wuzzy' immortalised by Rudyard Kipling. The Hadendowah were a sub-tribe of the Beja people and inhabited an area around Suakin.

with crescents and movable nasal guards, body armour - either cuirass or mail shirt - and ride fine Arab steeds. The saddles had high cantles and pommels, their bridles were decorated with brass studs and coloured horse hair. The horses' faces were covered with fly-fringing as were their rumps. Those emirs who had made the pilgrimage to Mecca wore green turbans.

The counter view is that such trappings represented a 'parade' uniform that would not be worn in the field. Instead, the emirs would wear a '*jibba*' (see below) to symbolise their piety. Usually, however attired, the emirs led their men on horseback.

The Beja - Beni-Amer, Bisharin and Hadendowah - of the eastern Sudan wore either ankle length loose white cotton trousers or a loin cloth and little else, apart from bead necklaces and amulets. The remaining tribes of pure Arab stock shaved their heads except for a single lock of hair and often wore a skull cap.

The Dervishes wore a sleeveless or short sleeved white cotton smock called a '*jibba*' (also, '*jibbeh*' or '*jibbah*') which hung down to the knees and had sleeves ending just below the wearer's elbow.

In the years up to 1885, it carried patches of red and dark blue, but later these could be black, blue, green, red, tan, or - occasionally - brown, sewn on the back, front and sleeves of the garment to symbolise the Mahdi's poverty. Coloured edging also decorated the hem, neck and sleeves.

The jibba was worn with close fitting cotton trousers, simple sandals, a girdle of plaited straw, a skull cap and a white turban, with one loose end hanging behind the wearer's left ear, and beads were additional items prescribed by the Mahdi.

The Baggara, Beja and Bisharin wore ankle length, once white, cotton trousers or loin cloths. Their hair frizzed out some six to eight inches (150-200mm) on each side of the head and it is these warriors who were the 'fuzzy-wuzzies' immortalised by the words of Rudyard Kipling.

Flags

The Dervish sub-divisions could be identified by means of their flags, with each Emir having their own as did the lesser commanders. The banners and flags were individually made, usually oblong in shape, four feet long by three feet wide. They could be black, blue, green, red or white, often with coloured borders and adorned with four line passages in Arabic from the Koran. The design was sometimes only on one side, with the reverse being left plain. The flag poles were often decorated with brass balls, crescents, globes and horse tails.

Weapons

The mainstay of Dervish weapons were the 10 feet long, broad bladed, thrusting spear and the similarly long, straight bladed, double edged sword with a simple cross hilt. Shorter and lighter throwing spears could be carried and also a hooked throwing stick used for bringing down camels and horses by being thrown at the animal's legs.

Many of the Bela and Bisharin carried hook bladed knives, held in a sheath worn on the upper arm.

The bulk of the shields were round and made from crocodile, elephant or rhinoceros hide, supposedly tough enough to deflect a bullet. There was also a number of wicker work oblong shields. There is some discussion concerning the extent to which the tribesmen actually used shields. The Beja, for example are thought to have favoured their use, whereas the Kordofan Arabs at least did not.

The emirs were armed with lances and curved swords and carried decorated shields. Some of the tribesmen, notably the 'Jehadia' were armed with locally made flintlocks, or old Remington rifles taken from the Egyptian garrison at El Obeid, or various other European rifles that had been captured. As the Mahdi's forces went from victory to victory - those over Colonel Hicks (Shaykan 1883) and General Baker (El Teb 1884) and for example - so the number of rifles and ammunition coming into their possession increased.

The Mahdi's forces had some artillery; at the time of Omdurman the Dervishes had a number of batteries, each of six guns. Stored in Omdurman, or sited in earthworks along the Nile were 63 guns - 35 brass mountain guns, eight Krupp guns, seven machine guns and 13 miscellaneous pieces. Not too much should be made of this, as only five guns were used by the Dervishes during the battle of Omdurman, all under the Black Flag, and their effectiveness seems to have been negligible. These pieces were manned by Egyptian gunners who were pressed into service. Ammunition was in short supply and locally made shells achieving a range of just 500 yards - as opposed to the typical 2,500 yards with the intended ammunition - did not help.

Another type of Beja tribesmen of the Sudan, who with the Hadendowah formed the swordsmen and spearmen of the Mahdi's army.

Hadendowah tribesman.

General Sir Herbert Stewart KGB (Bt). This officer served in the Sudan under General Graham and was present at the battles of El Teb and Tamai. (Courtesy John Young collection.)

The Gordon Relief Expedition 1884-1885

It was not until September 1884 once General Gordon's predicament in Khartoum became known in Great Britain that the British government relented in the face of public opinion . An expeditionary force to relieve Khartoum and rescue Gordon was authorised. General Sir Garnet Wolseley, who had led the 1882 Nile campaign was again placed in command and arrived in Cairo that same month. His force consisted of a cavalry regiment, a mountain artillery battery and eight battalions of infantry - 6,000 men, all drawn from the British troops already in Egypt.

Following discussion, often heated, it was decided that the route these troops would take to reach Khartoum was by rail as far as Sarrass and then via the River Nile. The river section of the journey would not be easy; over 800 miles, including traversing four all but impassable cataracts. Whaling boats, 800 in all, each 30 feet long, were to be specially constructed at various UK shipyards. On completion, these boats would be shipped to Alexandria and piloted down the Nile by boatmen from Canada ('voyageurs') and East Africa ('kraomen').

Due to the delays caused by the Prime Minister and the time taken to organise and convey a larger force, General Wolseley requested the formation at home of a camel mounted flying column to precede the main body of his force.

Volunteers were called for from the Household Cavalry and line cavalry regiments, the Foot Guards, rifle and line regiments. There was no shortage of volunteers and soon the Camel Corps was formed, embarking for Egypt on 26th September.

The whaling boats arrived in Egypt and on 6th November, civilian paddle steamers, used to tow them down the Nile as far as the first cataract, set off. Each boat carried 10 soldiers and two boatmen. Once the first cataract was reached, the whaling boats were moved overland around the obstacle by sheer hard labour then re-floated and rowed onwards.

Korti was reached on 15th December and a camp was established by Brigadier General Sir Herbert Stewart. Here General Wolseley, working on the information gained in a short message from Gordon, divided his force into two separate columns.

A 2,200 strong River Column under Major General Earle was to carry on down the Nile to Abu Hamed, then proceed overland to Korosko and then move on Berber.

A second column, the 'Desert Column', led by Brigadier Stewart would move south east across 150 miles of desert to Metemmeh to open a faster, more direct route to Khartoum.

At Metemmeh the two columns would link up for the final approach to Khartoum. Under orders from the British Government, Wolseley himself remained in Korti and did not travel with either force.

The River Column
Major General Earle commanding
Colonel Brackenbury second-in-command

- 1/The South Staffordshire Regiment (38th) (600)
- 2/The Essex Regiment (56th) (740)
- 1/The Duke of Cornwall's Light Infantry (32nd) (650)

- 1/The Black Watch (Royal Highland Regiment) (42nd) (675)
- 1/The Gordon Highlanders (75th) (750)
- 1/The Queen's Own (Royal West Kent Regiment) (50th) (750)
- 1/Princess Victoria's (Royal Irish Fusiliers) (87th) (750)
- 1/The Queen's Own Cameron Highlanders (79th) (500)
- 8th Railway Company RE
- 11th Field Company RE
- 26th Field Company RE
- Naval Brigade (57)
- 19th Hussars (350)
- Egyptian Camel Company (160)
- Egyptian Camel Battery (6 x 7pdrs) (120)
- Boatmen (370)
- Egyptian soldiers (hauling boats) (370)

The River Column used the river steamers belonging to the tourist operator Thomas Cook and Sons to move their men and supplies on the Nile as far as Wadi Halfa. Some of these towed the whaling boats, but once a cataract was reached, the steam boats were of no further use. From this point onwards it was sheer muscle power that moved the Column up the River Nile.

The Desert Column
Brigadier General Sir Herbert Stewart commanding

- Staff (8 officers + 6 other ranks)
- Guards Camel Regiment (21+336)
- Heavy Camel Regiment (24+376)
- Mounted Infantry Camel Regiment (21+336)
- 1/The Royal Sussex Regiment (35th) (16+401)
- 1/The Essex Regiment (3+55)
- 19th Hussars (2 squadrons) (9+121)
- 26th Field Company RE (part) (27)
- 1/1 Southern Divisional RA (part) (3 x 7pdr screw guns) (4+39)
- Naval Brigade (Including a Gardner gun) (5+53)
- Commissariat and Transport (5+72)
- Medical Staff (3+50)

Abu Klea 17th January 1885

On 30th December 1884 Brigadier Stewart led his Desert Column on the first leg of his journey across 150 miles of desert to Metemmeh. The first objective was the wells at Jakdul, some 90 miles south east of the British camp at Korti. The wells were reached on 12th January and, after leaving a detachment to guard them, Stewart moved on towards Abu Klea, the wells there offering the next supply of water. All his men were mounted on camels, apart from the 19th Hussars who rode horses.

During the afternoon of the second day of the march, natives were spotted around the flanks of the column and then directly across its path. Brigadier Stewart, not wishing to engage the enemy without a full day's light, made camp for the day. A zareba - a low hedge made from thorn bushes and reinforced by camel saddles and

Part of a contemporary illustration showing Brigadier Stewart (on horse) and Frederick Burnaby (centre, in dark patrol jacket) with Lord Dundonald of the Life Guards in the foreground, on the morning of the battle of Abu Klea.

stores - was built around the camp as a safety measure. It was nightfall before this work was completed.

As the column formed up for the next days march, it came under sniper fire and, taking this as a prelude to an attack, Brigadier Stewart formed his command into a single large square. The three outer ranks were formed from the infantry, with the transport camels and artillery in the centre of the square and some mounted infantry out-stationed as skirmishers.

Moving in such a formation was slow work, with frequent stops in order to maintain the cohesion of the square, all carried out in searing heat.

A line of flags across the line of march was seen ahead and as the square stopped yet again to correct dressing, perhaps 200 yards from the flags, it was seen that they were being carried by an army of around 11,000 tribesmen, led by the Emir of Berber and the Emir of Metemmeh.

The tribesmen were 4,000-6,000 Duguaim, Kenana and Hamr Arabs from Kordofan, led by Sheik Musa, Emir of the Hamr Arabs. The Ja-alin and 2,000 Metammeh men under Ali Wad Saad, Emir of Metammeh were kept in reserve and the Awadiyeh formed the scouting cavalry. There were 2,000 Ababdeh, Bisharin and other Arabs from Berber under Abd al-Majid, the nephew of the Emir of Berber and 60 soldiers from the old Egyptian army. Also present were 1,000 men (400 with rifles) from the Mahdi's Khartoum army who were to carry out the main attack on the British.

Driven on by incessant drum beats, wave after wave of swiftly moving tribesmen flung themselves at the left face of the square, only to be laid low by rifle and machine gun fire. The rear corner of the square that was temporarily out of dressing was also attacked. Here the situation quickly became critical as a Gardner gun - sited at the left

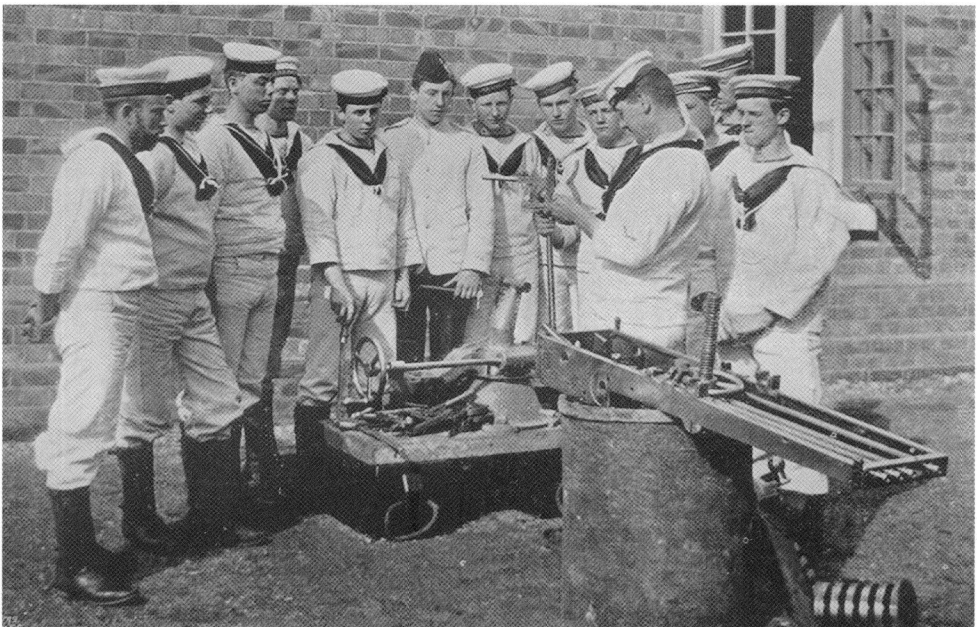

A group of naval ratings being instructed on the mechanics of the Gardner gun. The white hot climate uniform would have been worn in the Sudan, the naval cap being replaced by a Foreign Service helmet, plus equipment.

BATTLE OF ABU KLEA

17th January 1885

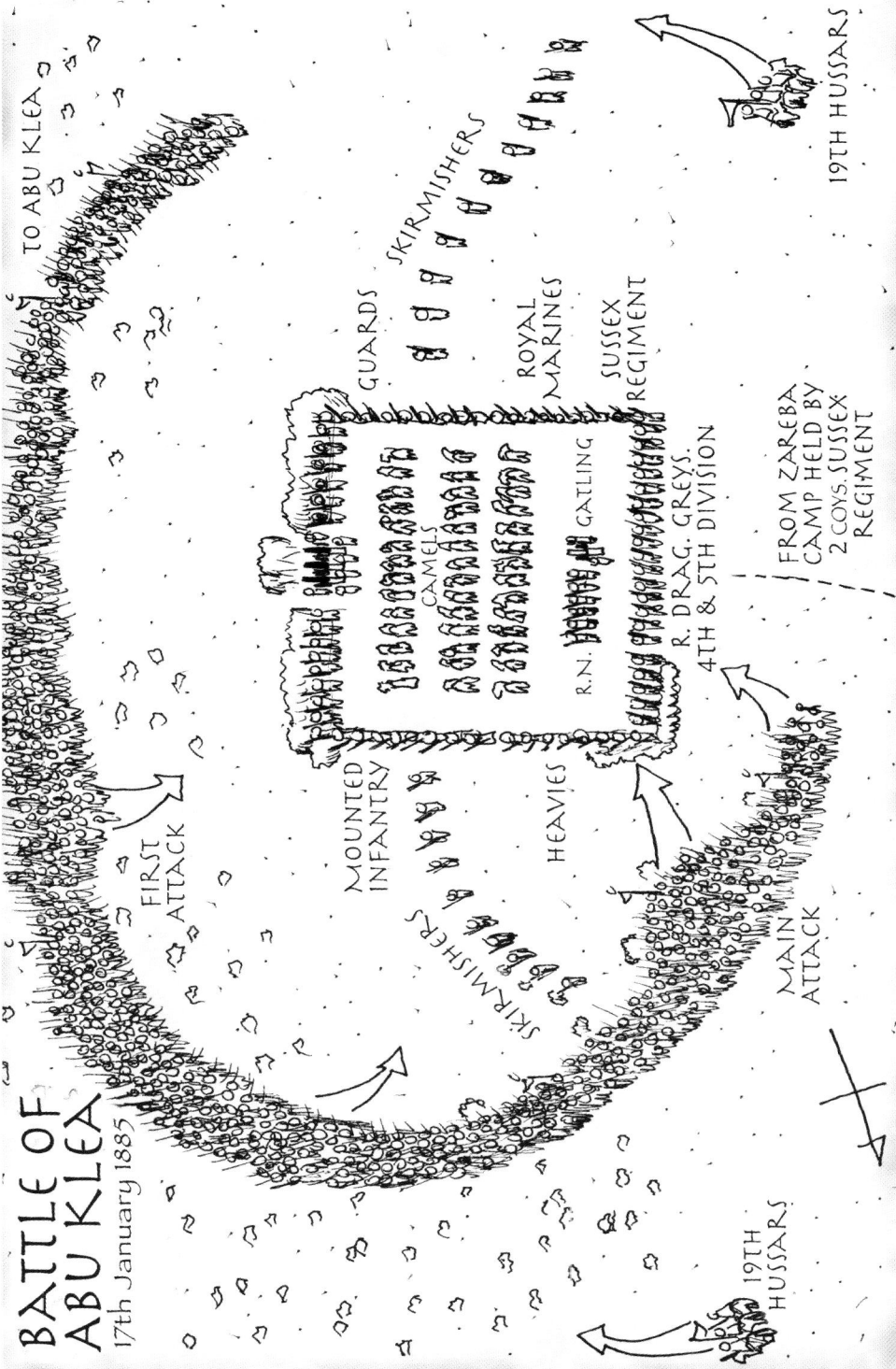

TO ABU KLEA

GUARDS

SKIRMISHERS

ROYAL MARINES

SUSSEX REGIMENT

CAMELS

R.N. GATLING

R. DRAG. GREYS.
4TH & 5TH DIVISION

FROM ZAREBA CAMP HELD BY 2 COYS. SUSSEX REGIMENT

19TH HUSSARS

MOUNTED INFANTRY

SKIRMISHERS

HEAVIES

FIRST ATTACK

MAIN ATTACK

19TH HUSSARS

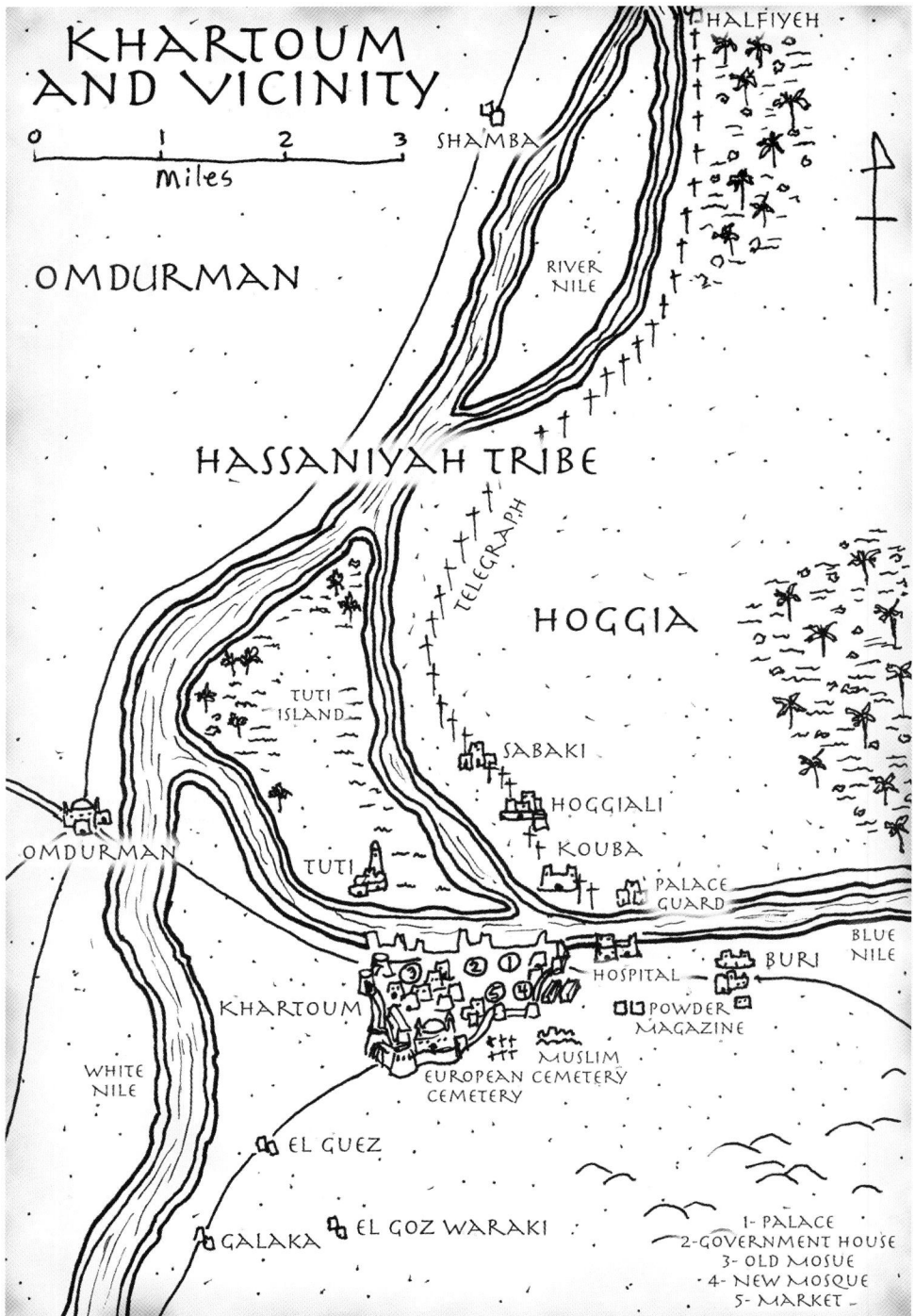

KHARTOUM AND VICINITY

0 1 2 3
Miles

OMDURMAN

SHAMBA

HALFIYEH

RIVER NILE

HASSANIYAH TRIBE

TELEGRAPH

HOGGIA

TUTI ISLAND

SABAKI

HOGGIALI

KOUBA

OMDURMAN

TUTI

PALACE GUARD

BLUE NILE

HOSPITAL

BURI

KHARTOUM

POWDER MAGAZINE

WHITE NILE

MUSLIM CEMETERY

EUROPEAN CEMETERY

EL GUEZ

EL GOZ WARAKI

GALAKA

1- PALACE
2- GOVERNMENT HOUSE
3- OLD MOSUE
4- NEW MOSQUE
5- MARKET

rear corner to cover a deliberate break in the lines made to permit the skirmishers to fall back - jammed and many sailors became casualties. As a result, number of tribesmen got into the square through the gap. Brigadier Stewart had his horse shot from under him and rifle after rifle jammed as a result of rapid firing in the fierce heat of the desert.

The British troops fought hand to hand with the tribesmen. The front and right faces of the square that had not as yet come under attack stood firm, which aided the square's cohesion. Those faces under attack gave ground under pressure and gradually what had been the centre of the square became a mass of fighting men. The transport camels that had been positioned in the centre provided a living barrier that both impeded the impetus of the tribesmen and provided the British with some respite in which to re-organise.

The rear ranks of the unengaged faces of the square turned about and poured heavy fire at the natives that had broken into the formation. With close range rifle fire smashing into their ranks, the tribesmen suffered heavy casualties and broke off the fighting as swiftly as they had attacked.

In a fiercely fought action that lasted only minutes, seven officers and 85 other ranks were wounded, with perhaps 1,000 tribesmen being killed.

Abu Kru 19th January 1885

After spending the night at Abu Klea, Brigadier Stewart left a small garrison and began to march on to Metemmeh on the banks of the Nile and some 25 miles distant.

After a days uninterrupted progress, a large force of tribesmen was observed between the column and their destination.

Brigadier Stewart halted his men and allowed them a meal before moving on. The Brigadier was mortally wounded by a sniper during the halt.

Command of the Desert Column passed to Colonel Sir Charles Wilson KCMG RE, an intelligence officer and deputy adjutant general of the relief expedition. Leaving some troops in a hastily constructed camp, Colonel Wilson moved the rest of his command towards the Nile.

Forming his men into a square, Colonel Wilson soon came under attack from tribesmen.

The fire power from the square hit the oncoming tribesmen, suffering heavy casualties and with their front ranks continually being swept away, the natives turned and ran.

The Nile is Reached

The men in Colonel Wilson's square reached the Nile and camped on the river's banks for the night. The next day they retraced their steps and the re-formed column moved on.

On 21st January, Colonel Wilson made an unsuccessful attempt to take the well defended town of Metemmeh, two miles away. After being joined by three armoured river steamboats that Gordon had sent from Khartoum filled with Sudanese soldiers, Colonel Wilson spent the next few days fuelling the steamboats and reconoitering the river. After losing four days, he moved down the Nile towards Khartoum with two of the steamboats, the *Bordein* and the *Talahawiyeh*.

Coming under increasingly heavy fire, the steamers carried on, but when

Khartoum was neared on 28th January, it was clear from the lack of Egyptian flags - one always flew over Gordon's headquarters - that the town had fallen. Ironically, the approach of the relieving forces had urged the Mahdi's forces onto one final effort; Khartoum had been stormed on 26th January and Gordon had been killed.

The Fall of Khartoum

Despite weak fortifications, insufficient food and an under strength garrison, Gordon withstood the siege for 317 days. At the end, with ammunition and food supplies exhausted, the impoverished and disheartened garrison could do little to fend off the last determined assault by the Mahdi's forces.

The relief force arrived two days after Gordon's death on 26th January 1885. As the news of the fall of Khartoum spread, the men in the relief columns were dispirited as their mission was now without purpose. Further, all the Mahdist forces that had been involved in the attacks on the city were now available to take the field.

The British government, highly unpopular once the death of Gordon became public knowledge, gave General Wolseley three new objectives; the final destruction of the Mahdi, the construction of a railway southwards from Berber and the mounting of another expedition against Osman Digna.

Since the original mission had been to relieve Khartoum, Wolseley felt that he needed reinforcements to take on the Mahdi's forces, but in the time it would take for such reinforcements to arrive, he felt able to deal with the Government's other instructions.

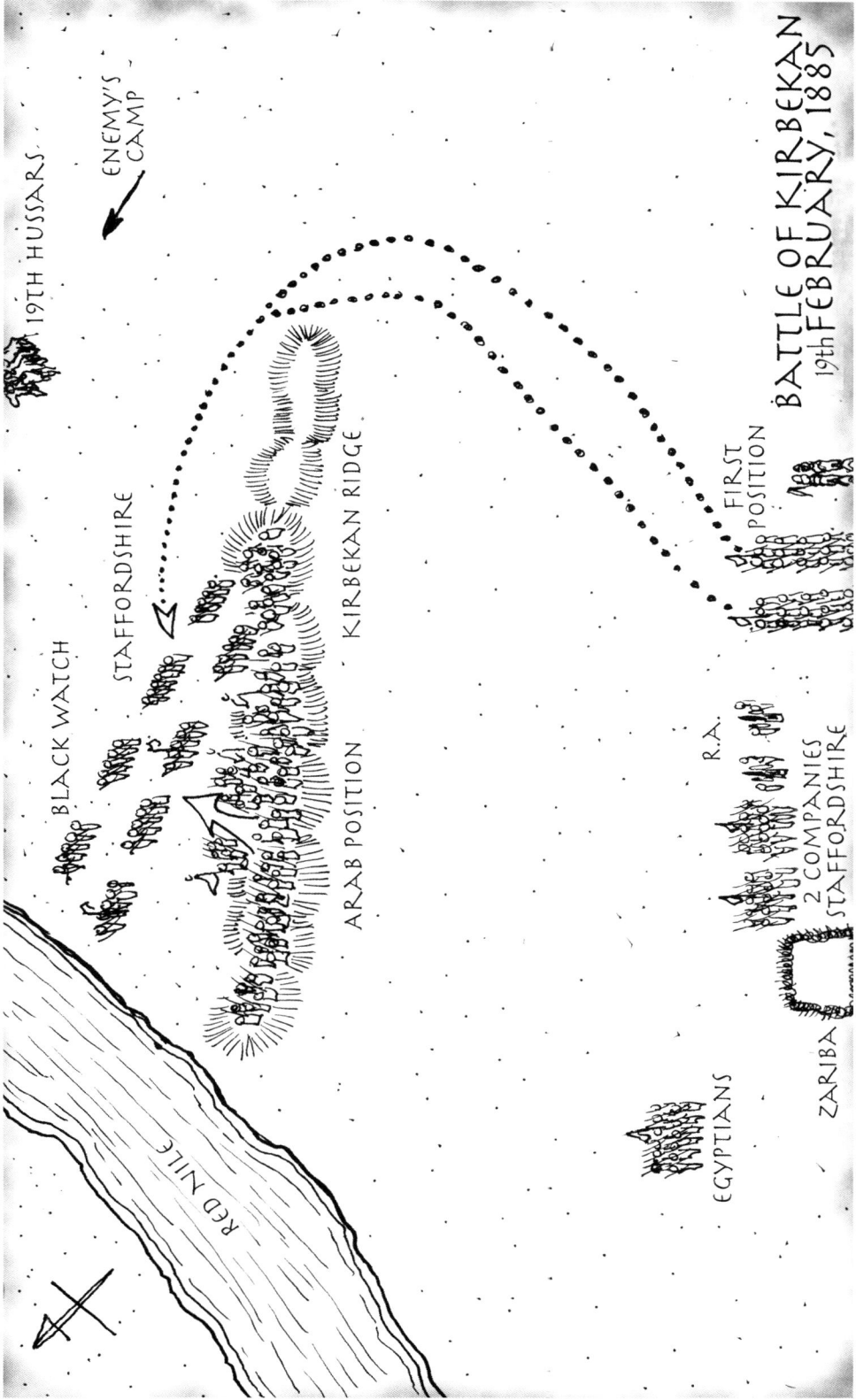

BATTLE OF KIRBEKAN
19th FEBRUARY, 1885

19TH HUSSARS

ENEMY'S CAMP

STAFFORDSHIRE

BLACK WATCH

KIRBEKAN RIDGE

ARAB POSITION

FIRST POSITION

R.A.

2 COMPANIES
STAFFORDSHIRE

ZARIBA

EGYPTIANS

RED NILE

33

THE MARCH TO EL TEB

28th – 29th FEBRUARY, 1884

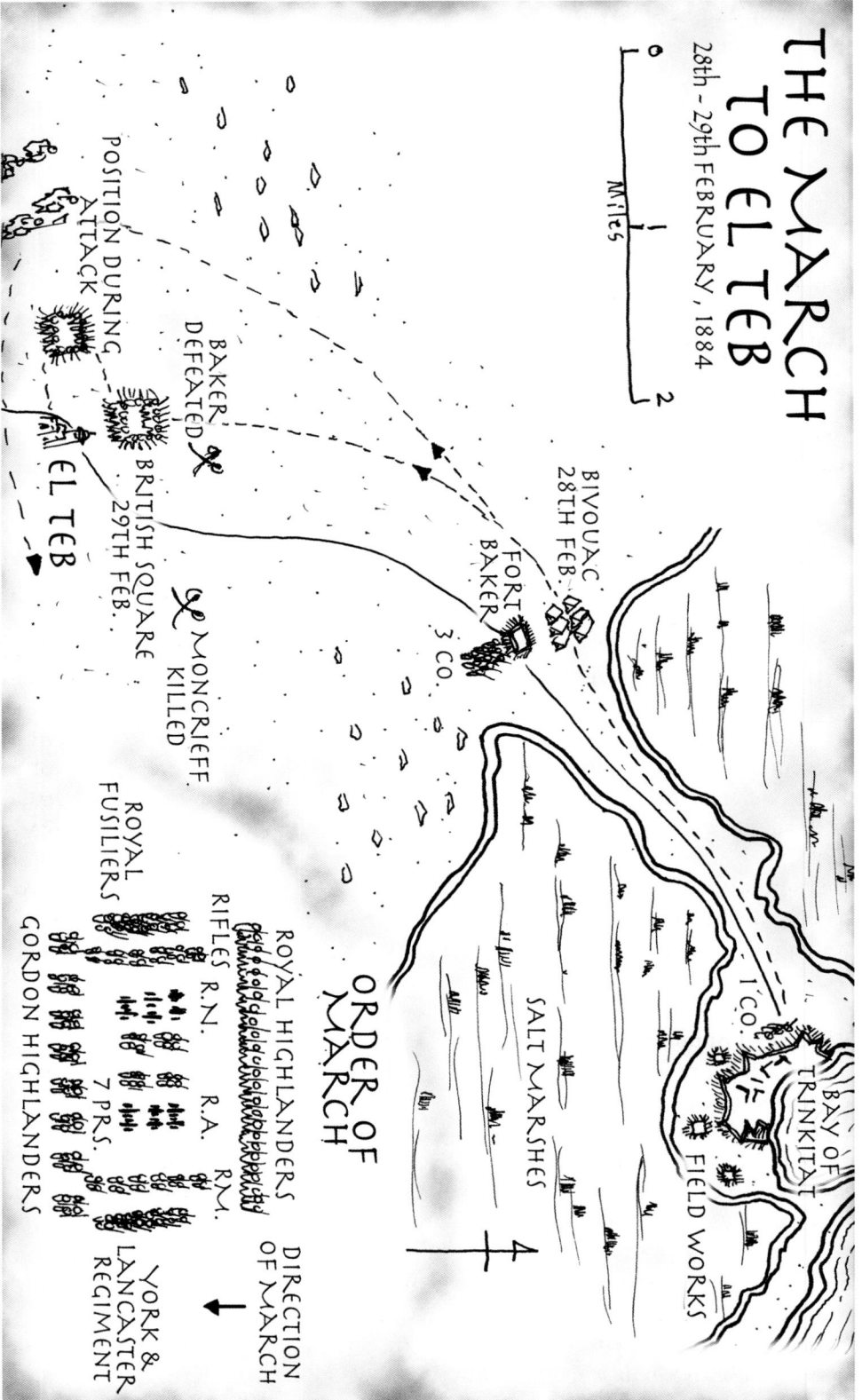

Miles

0 1 2

BIVOUAC
28TH FEB.

FORT
BAKER

3 CO.

BAKER
DEFEATED

POSITION DURING
ATTACK

BRITISH SQUARE
29TH FEB.

EL TEB

MONCRIEFF
KILLED

SALT MARSHES

1 CO.

FIELD WORKS

BAY OF
TRINKITAT

ORDER OF MARCH

DIRECTION
OF MARCH

ROYAL HIGHLANDERS

RIFLES R.N. R.A. R.M.

7 PRS.

ROYAL
FUSILIERS

GORDON HIGHLANDERS

YORK &
LANCASTER
REGIMENT

Kirbekan 19th February 1885

Major General Sir Redvers Henry Buller VC, Chief of Staff to Wolseley, was sent to assume command of the Desert Column in place of the mortally wounded General Stewart.

On 10th February 1885 General Wolseley ordered the Desert Column to Metemmeh in order to liaise with the River Column and take Berber - a necessary step in the construction of a railway southwards from that town.

The River Column under Major General Earle had been making slow progress and was some 200 miles away from Berber. Under General Wolseley's orders the Column continued down the Nile towards Abu Hamed, 30 miles away.

Scouts of the 19th Hussars operating from the Column detected a large force of Arabs occupying a line of low hills. This was supported by more tribesmen to the rear, positioned on a higher ridge called the Jebel Kirbekan.

Although most of his men were some way behind him, General Earle decided to attack these positions. He had with him a squadron of the 19th Hussars, 1/South Staffordshire Regiment, 1/The Black Watch, an Egyptian camel company and an Egyptian camel battery.

Supported by two pieces of artillery, two companies from the South Staffordshire Regiment landed and advanced against the first enemy positions. A flanking movement along a concealed wadi was conducted by the rest of the infantry, covered by the 19th Hussars and the camel company.

Lieutenant Colonel P H Eyre was killed leading two companies of his South Staffordshire Regiment against the higher, rearmost enemy ridge and his command became pinned down.

As the flanking force rounded the flank of the highest enemy position it was seen and came under heavy fire. The Black Watch, supported by the remainder of the South Staffords attacked the rear of the first enemy position and was in turn charged by Arab spearmen. The men of the Black Watch contained this attack, but General Earle was killed. Colonel Henry Brackenbury, Deputy Assistant Adjutant and Quartermaster of the Relief Expedition and Earle's second in command took over, sending the infantry to clear the enemy from the ridge and relieve the troops who were pinned down. This was achieved at bayonet point - a more numerous enemy had been evicted from a strong position and comprehensively defeated.

Wolseley's Summer Camp

General Buller moved to command the Desert Column at Gubat and found his new command to be badly spent and marched them to Abu Klea where he established camp.

This news, plus the continued slow progress of the River Column caused General Wolseley to cancel immediate operations on 20th February and recall his men back to Korti on the River Nile, about 150 miles north west of Berber.

Here a camp was established with the intention of the troops awaiting the relatively cooler autumn weather before beginning another campaign.

It was at this point that the British Government decided to withdraw all its forces from the Sudan and concentrate them in Egypt. Russian moves in Afghanistan threatened British India and a war with Russia looked eminently possible.

Despite protests from General Wolseley, by now in Cairo and working on the plan for a renewed offensive against the Mahdi, this move went ahead and the troops were withdrawn.

As a result, the Mahdi was left in full control of the entire Sudan, but he died from typhus on 20th June 1885 without being able to benefit from his victories.

The task of establishing a government fell to the Mahdi's three deputies, or caliphs, chosen by him. There was great rivalry between the three caliphs and all three - each supported by the inhabitants of his particular native region - continued squabbling until 1891 when Abdullah Ibn Mohammed overcame the opposition of the other two and emerged unchallenged as leader of the Mahdiyah. Entitled the Khalifa or 'successor', Abdullah el-Taaishi, he purged the Mahdiyah of members of the Mahdi's family and many of his early religious disciples and was to dominate Sudan for the next 13 years.

The Battle of Ginnis 30th December 1885

The Khalifa moved his army up to the Egyptian border and engaged an Anglo-Egyptian force guarding the frontier at a reinforced outpost near Wadi Halfa, manned by a detachment of the Queen's Own Cameron Highlanders and two Sudanese infantry companies. Lieutenant General Sir F Stephenson arrived with reinforcements from Cairo and counter attacked the Mahdist forces at Ginnis on 30th December. Stephenson's victory was complete and the Khalifa's first foray against Egypt was brought to an abrupt halt.

British Order of Battle, Ginnis 30th December 1885
Lieutenant General Sir F Stephenson

- 1/Princess Charlotte of Wales's (Royal Berkshire Regiment) (*)
- 1/The Queen's Own (Royal West Kent Regiment
- 1/The Princess of Wales's Own (Yorkshire Regiment)
- 2/The Durham Light Infantry

(* = the prefix 'Royal' had been granted by Queen Victoria following the Battalion's brave stand at Tofrek 22 March 1885)

This action brought a full stop to the 1885 campaign.

Three of the British infantry battalions that took part in the action were destined to be the last British soldiers to wear scarlet tunics in action. The troops were ordered '*to put on our red serges as it was thought the force would look more formidable to the Dervishes dressed in red than in khakee*' (Captain Ferrer 1/The Princess of Wales's Own (Yorkshire Regiment)). Only the Durham Light Infantry remained in khaki.

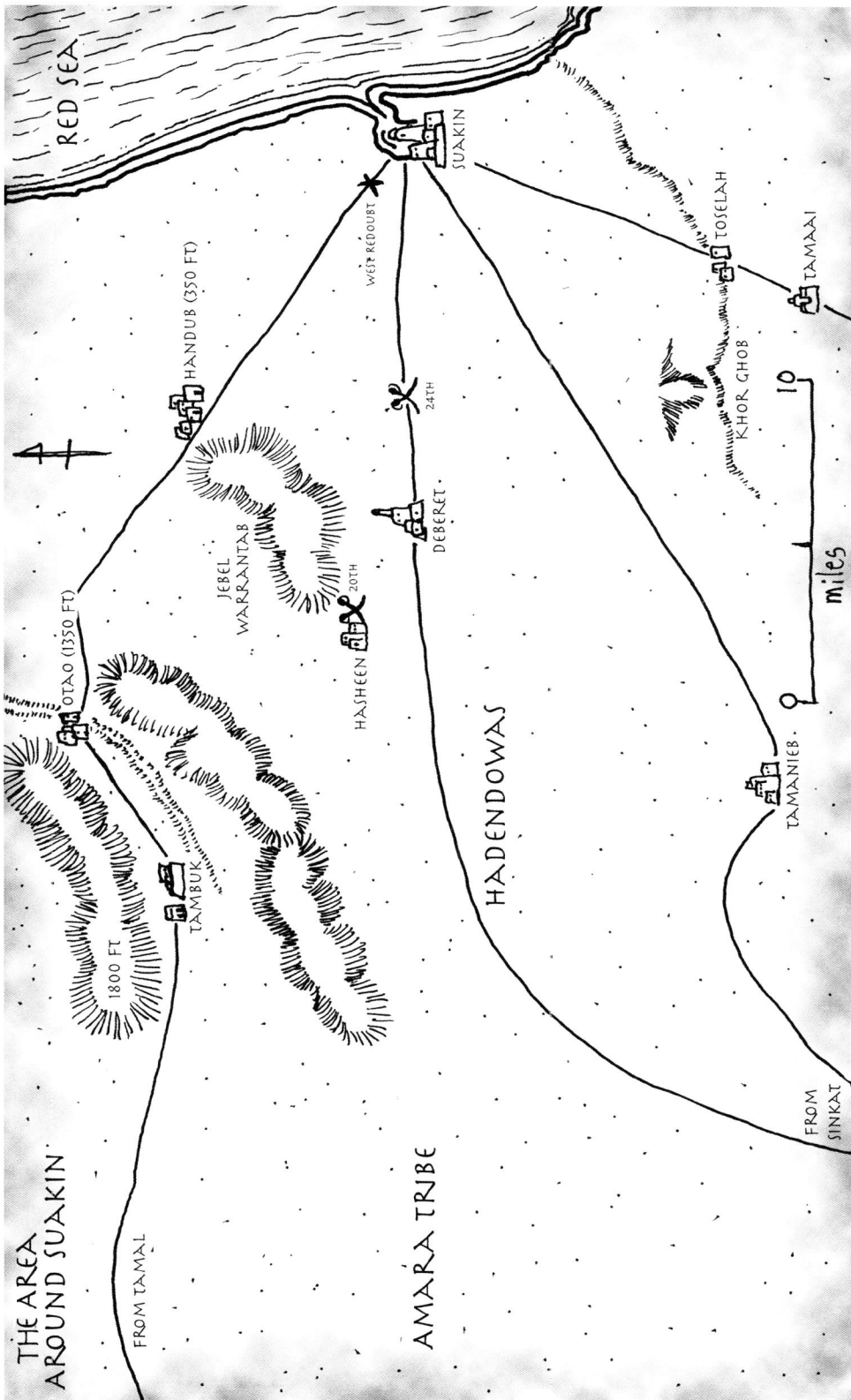

THE AREA
AROUND SUAKIN

RED SEA

SUAKIN

WEIR REDOUBT

HANDUB (350 FT)

JEBEL
WARRANTAB

OTAO (350 FT)

24TH

DEBBEH

20TH

HASHEEN

TAMBUK

1800 FT

HADENDOWAS

AMARA TRIBE

FROM TAMAL

FROM SINKAT

TAMANIEB

TOSELAH

TAMAAI

KHOR GHOB

10

miles

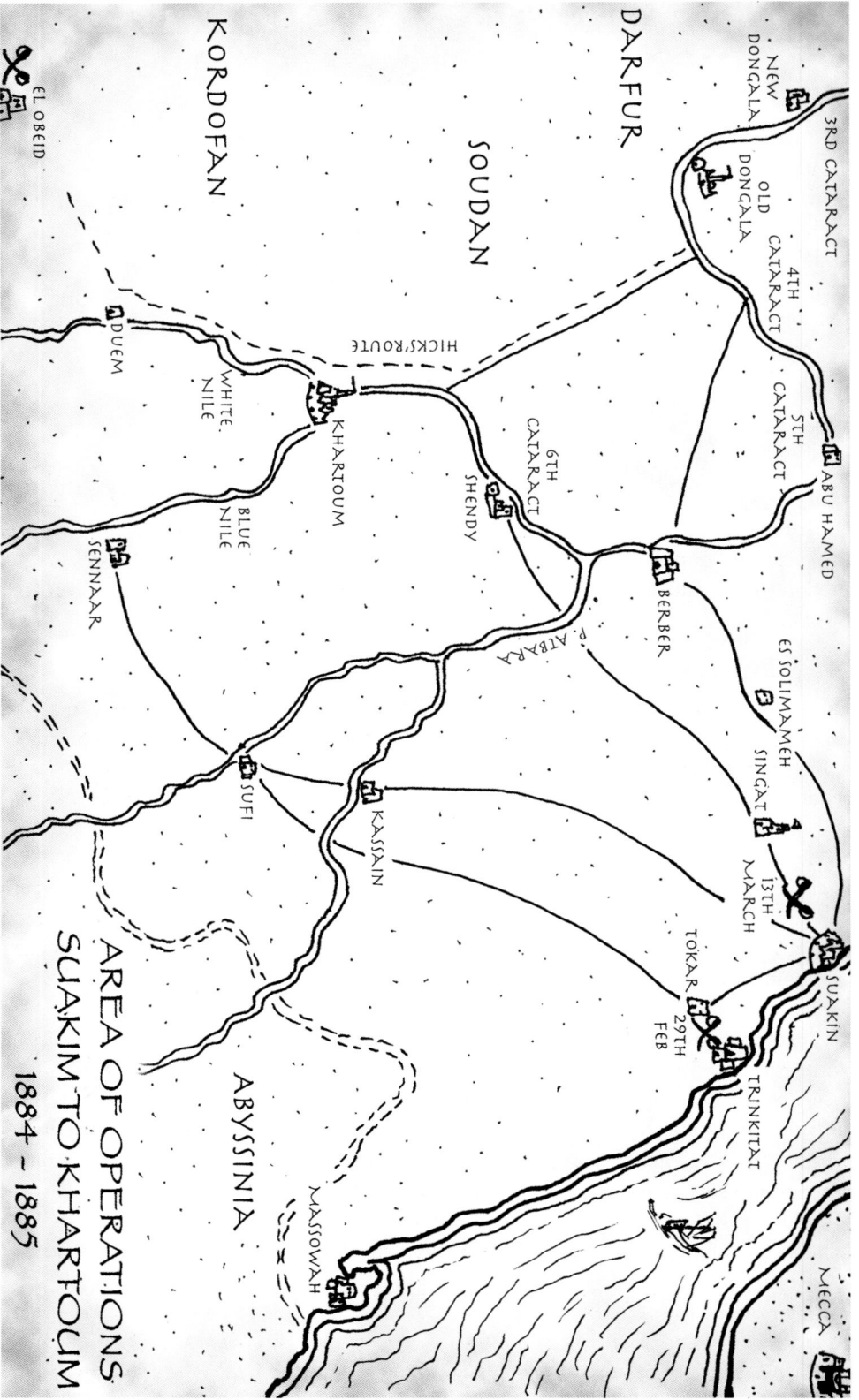

AREA OF OPERATIONS
SUAKIM TO KHARTOUM
1884 ~ 1885

DARFUR

KORDOFAN

SOUDAN

EL OBEID

NEW DONGALA

OLD DONGALA

3RD CATARACT

4TH CATARACT

5TH CATARACT

6TH CATARACT

HICKS' ROUTE

DUEM

WHITE NILE

KHARTOUM

SHENDY

BLUE NILE

SENNAAR

ABU HAMED

BERBER

R. ATBARA

ES SOLIMAMEH

SINGAT

13TH MARCH

SUFI

KASSAIN

TOKAR

29TH FEB

SUAKIN

TRINKITAT

ABYSSINIA

MASSOWAH

MECCA

The Expeditions Against Osman Digna
1884-1885

The First Expedition 1884

Uthman Ben Abu Bakr Digna, better known as Osman Digna was a Beja-Hadendowah slave trader operating in the Red Sea around the port of Suakin. The Mahdi had appointed Osman Digna as his lieutenant and made him Emir of Eastern Sudan. Digna's first act was to lay siege to Sinkat, some 60 miles from Suakin.

The Red Sea port of Suakin is situated on an island near the end of a narrow inlet, 12 miles long and approximately two miles wide. The British considered the place to be important - a point not lost on Digna.

The fates of Colonel Hicks and General Baker served to underline the fact that there was a need for regular troops to be deployed.

Royal Marines from a naval squadron under Admiral Sir William Hewitt VC KCB anchored off Suakin came ashore and secured the vital port on 10th February. On the 12th, General Stephenson in Cairo was ordered to send troops from Egypt to Suakin (19th Hussars, 1/Black Watch, 1/Gordon Highlanders, 3/King's Royal Rifle Corps) under Major General Graham VC CB RE while more soldiers on their way back to England from India (10th Hussars, 1/York and Lancaster Regiment, 2/ Royal Irish Fusiliers) were diverted to the area.

The Battle of El Teb, 29th February 1884

On 23rd February Major General Sir Gerald Graham VC was given command of an expedition against Osman Digna. Six days later he marched out of Trinkitat with his 4,300 troops, heading towards El Teb, where it was understood that 10,000-12,000 rebels were encamped on the ground near where General Baker's men had fallen - and, it transpired - their bodies still lying out in the open.

General Graham's men approached the enemy position formed into one large square; on the march the front and rear faces of the square moved in company column of fours, at company intervals, while the flanking formations moved in open column of companies. Intervals were left at the angles of the square for the guns and machine guns, with the Naval Brigade occupying the front, and the Royal Artillery the rear angles.

The square was covered by detachments of the 10th Hussars, and 19th Hussars, with the main force of the cavalry being in the rear under Brigadier Stewart.

As the square came within 200 yards of the natives, they charged the formation at break neck speed. The Dervishes seemed impervious to bullet wounds and many fell within five yards of the British lines. The natives charged again and again, but not one reached the square, as they were swept away by rifle fire.

On the other side of the square, contact was made and fierce hand to hand fighting ensued, but the Gardner guns of the Naval Brigade came into action and the assault was repelled.

The square formation was abandoned, the flank formations deployed and the advance continued in two long lines. The infantry encountered stiff opposition, as the Dervishes contested every yard of ground, but supported by artillery, began to clear

A contemporary illustration depicting the heroic lone fight of Private Edwards of the Black Watch to save the mules carrying the ammunition and winning his Victoria Cross at the battle of Tamai.

British and native officers of the 9th Bengal Cavalry, Suakin 1885.

the rebels from their entrenched positions in the village of El Teb and its wells. By 2pm the action was over, the village and its wells were carried and the natives were seen fleeing towards Tokar and Suakin.

The Battle of Tamai, 13th March 1884

Learning that Osman Digna's force was in position near the village and wells of Tamai, General Graham moved out from camp on 13th March with his force this time deployed into two squares, each a brigade strong and echeloned some 1,000 yards apart, with cavalry on their left flank. The squares moved steadily on over a route intersected by dry water courses, towards a deep hollow, full of rugged rocks and boulders.

The leading British square (1/Black Watch, 1/York and Lancaster, Royal Marines and Naval Brigade) commanded Major General Davis was attacked by swarms of tribesmen who emerged from the hollow and who seemed impervious to rifle, machine gun and artillery fire and made wild and furious rushes on the bayonets of the front ranks.

In the resultant smoke and din of battle, some confusion arose as Dervishes crept under cover of the smoke and flung their bare bodies onto the British bayonets and perished with dreadful wounds. The companies of the Black Watch and York and Lancaster Regiment that formed the front face of the leading square pressed forward, but the remaining companies of these battalions, which formed the sides of the square, and were also expecting an attack, did not keep up with the movement of those to the front and gaps appeared in the square.

41

The tribesmen broke into the square through these gaps as the rifle fire drowned out the frantic commands to close up. The York and Lancaster companies fell back onto the Royal Marines, firing as they went, with both units becoming intermingled. The Black Watch companies were thrown into some confusion and the leading square no longer existed. The soldiers split into small groups and there were many acts of valour and heroism as they sought to drive the natives back and prevent the artillery and machine guns from being captured.

The second British square under Major General Redvers Buller (Royal Irish Fusiliers, Gordon Highlanders, King's Royal Rifle Corps and Royal Marine Light Infantry) was about 500 yards away and was also under attack. Here however the sheer volume of firepower beat off the tribesmen and the men in the square were able to bring fire on to the flank of the natives attacking the other square. This was supported by fire on the enemy's other flank, provided by the dismounted cavalry.

The first square managed to regain some semblance of order before another native attack swept in from the ravine. The enemy attack wavered and as General Buller's men remained in square, the 2nd Brigade deployed into line and moved across it, covered by the 1st Brigade.

The 2nd Brigade advanced towards a ridge some 800 yards distant and this objective was carried, the troops firing as they moved on towards the Dervish main body gathered on the opposite ridge, which was also carried.

In the valley of Tamai Ghob, some 180 feet below, could be seen the tents and huts of the camp of Osman Digna, with the loot from all his previous victories.

General Graham reformed his men with the intention of advancing to some wells which were three miles away, and from where parties of Dervishes were still visible.

As the advance resumed, the natives moved as if to once again attack the squares. The halt was sounded and the British artillery dispersed the natives; the action was at an end. The Mahdi's general in command during the battle was Mahmoud Mousa, a cousin of Osman Digna who had fled to the hills.

British losses were five officers and 86 other ranks killed, eight officers and 103 other ranks wounded, with 18 missing men subsequently found amongst the fallen. The Dervishes losses in the action are thought to be around 2,000 out of an estimated 9,000.

General Buller's brigade demolished Osman Digna's camp while General Davis's weary troops marched back to the camp they had occupied the previous night.

After the action, General Graham was ordered back to Suakin and Osman Digna immediately took control of the area.

The Second Expedition 1885
After the battle of Kirbekan more troops were sent out from both home and India and a 13,000 strong force arrived in the British held Red Sea port of Suakin on 12th March 1885. The intention was that these troops under Lieutenant General Sir Gerald Graham VC would protect the construction of the Suakin to Berber railway as well bringing Osman Digna to book.

Following the fall of Khartoum, General Graham was given a three fold mission; to defeat Osman Digna, to take and hold the country astride the proposed Suakin-Berber railway route and to eventually link up with General Wolseley at Berber.

The Battle of Tamai, 13th March 1884

FORMATIONS
DURING THE BATTLE OF TAMAI
13th MARCH.1884

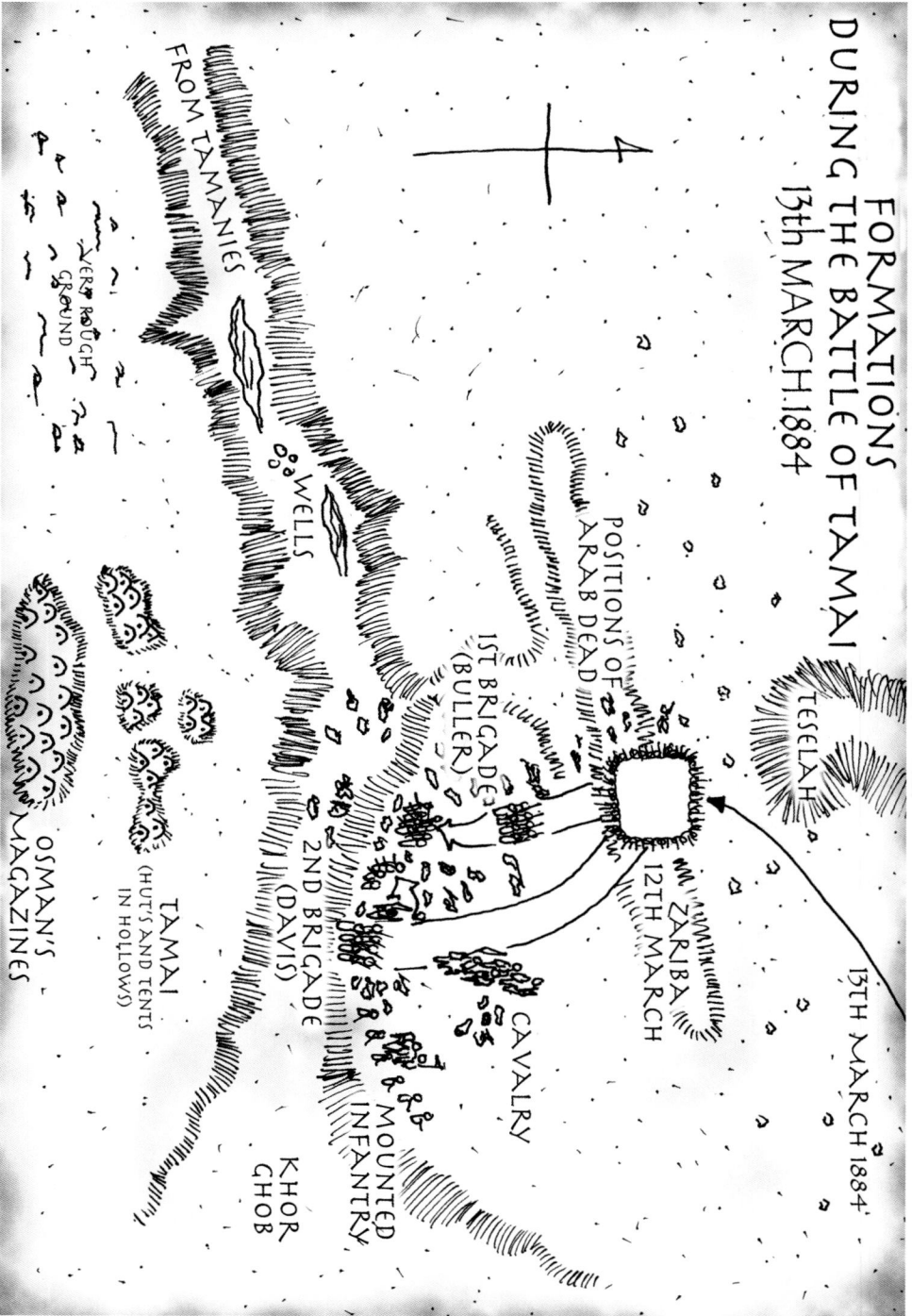

FROM TAMANIES

VERY ROUGH
GROUND

WELLS

POSITIONS OF
ARAB DEAD

1ST BRIGADE
(BULLER)

TESELAH

OSMAN'S
MAGAZINES

TAMAI
(HUTS AND TENTS
IN HOLLOW)

2ND BRIGADE
(DAVIS)

ZARIBA
12TH MARCH

CAVALRY

13TH MARCH 1884

KHOR
CHOB

MOUNTED
INFANTRY

The Second Expedition Against Osman Digna

Lieutenant General Sir Gerald Graham VC

Guards Brigade (Major General Lyon Fremantle)
- 1/Coldstream Guards (840)
- 2/Scots Guards (840)
- 3/Coldstream Guards (834)
- New South Wales Contingent (546)

2 Infantry Brigade (Major General Sir John McNeill VC KCB)
- 1/Princess Charlotte of Wales's (Berkshire Regiment) (650)
- 1/The King's (Shropshire Light Infantry) (800)
- 2/The East Surrey Regiment (600)
- Royal Marine Light Infantry (500)

Indian Brigade (Brigadier General J Hudson CB)
- 15th Ludhiana Sikhs (725)
- 17th Bengal Native Infantry (843)
- 28th Bombay Native Infantry (245)
- 'F' Company, Madras Sappers and Miners (150)

Cavalry Brigade (Major General Sir Henry Ewart KCB)
- 5th (Royal Irish) Lancers (2 Squadrons) (248)
- 20th Hussars (2 Squadrons) (261)
- 9th Bengal Cavalry (Hodson's Horse) (581)
- Mounted Infantry (4 Companies) (196)
- Mounted Infantry Police (13)

Artillery
- G/B RHA (6x9pdrs)
- 5/1 Scottish Division RA (6x2.5" screw guns)
- 6/1 Ammunition Column, Scottish Division RA

Royal Engineers
- 11th Company (attached to Mounted Infantry)
- 17th Company (105)
- 24th Company (124)
- 10th Railway Company
- 2nd and 3rd Sections, Telegraph Battalion
- Balloon Detachment
- 3, 5, 12 and 17 Companies, Commissariat and Transport Corps

Concentrating his force on Suakin, Graham believed the enemy to be in two main bodies, one at Tamai and the second at Hasheen, 10 miles west of Suakin. Since the tribesmen at Hasheen could potentially interfere with any moves against Tamai, Graham decided to tackle these first.

British and native officers of the 15th Ludhiana Sikhs. At Tofrek, the regiment stoutly defended the west face of the zareba, protecting the rear of the Berkshire Regiment.

Hasheen 20th March 1885

On 19th March 1885, General Graham marched his men out of Suakin towards the wells at Hasheen. The force was formed as three sides of an open square with the pack animals - camels and mules - in the centre and cavalry covering the front and flanks. At the end of the day's march the troops saw Dervishes occupying a strong position on a steep ridge to the square's left front and two battalions 1/Princess Charlotte of Wales's (Berkshire Regiment) and the Royal Marine Light Infantry were ordered to drive the natives from this position. The Indian 9th Bengal Cavalry charged the Dervishes, but were roughly handled by the tribesmen. The Indian infantry brigade, fighting in square with the Foot Guards inflicted heavy casualties, repulsing one Dervish attack and preventing another. The cavalry and mounted infantry made a successful attack, with the men firing their carbines as the Dervishes who had thrown themselves onto the ground to avoid the cavalry's swords. Still the natives fought on and General Graham's men fought and marched for over nine hours before the assaults petered out. It was calculated that the Dervish losses were between 250 and 1,000 while the Anglo-Indian force lost 22 all ranks killed and another 43 wounded.

A decisive victory had eluded General Graham's men, but a number of small redoubts, garrisoned by British infantry, were established on the ridge formerly occupied by the Dervishes.

BATTLE OF HASHEEN 20th MARCH, 1885

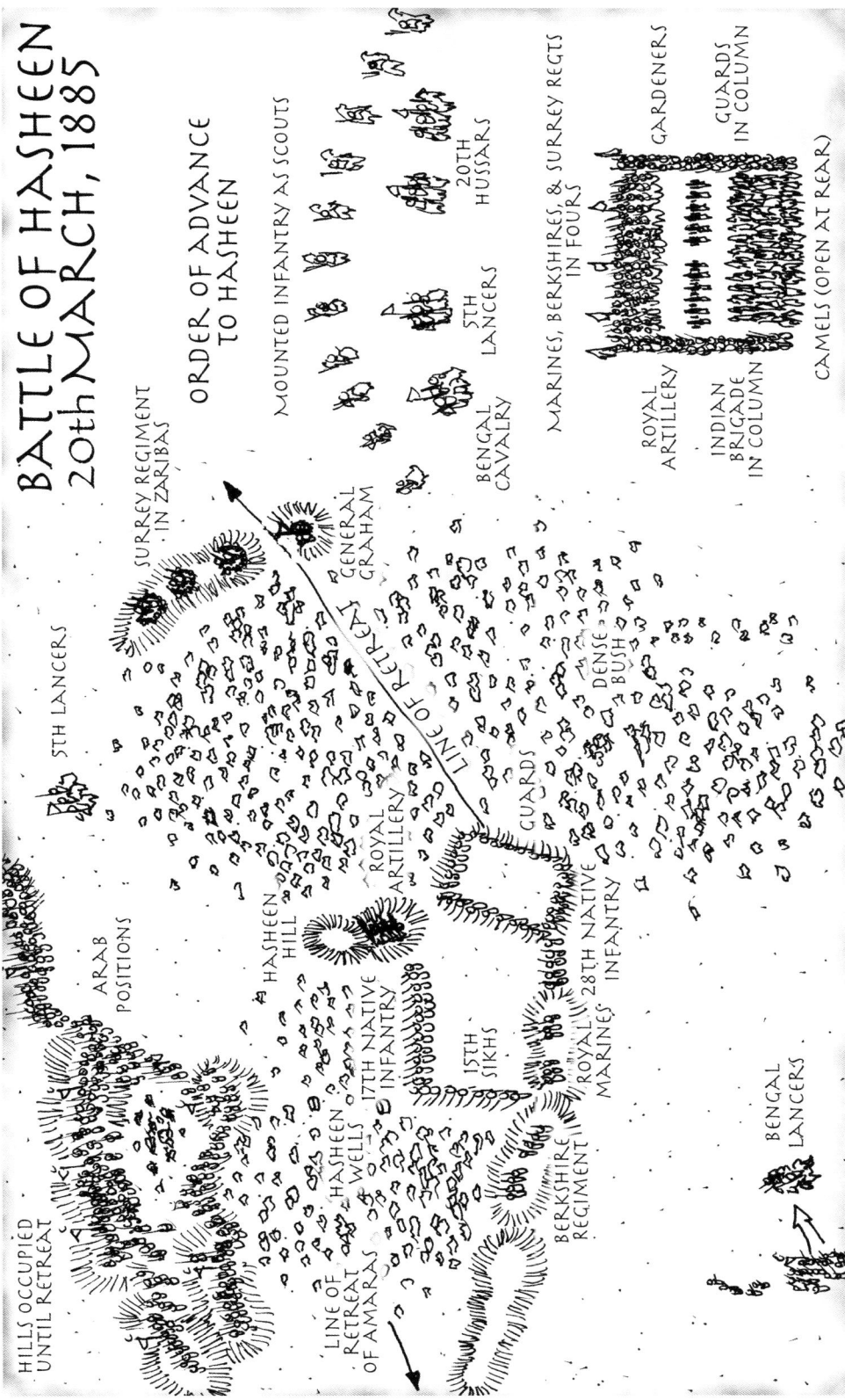

ORDER OF ADVANCE TO HASHEEN

MOUNTED INFANTRY AS SCOUTS

20TH HUSSARS

5TH LANCERS

BENGAL CAVALRY

MARINES, BERKSHIRES, & SURREY REGTS IN FOURS

GARDENERS

GUARDS IN COLUMN

ROYAL ARTILLERY

INDIAN BRIGADE IN COLUMN

CAMELS (OPEN AT REAR)

SURREY REGIMENT IN ZARIBAS

GENERAL GRAHAM

5TH LANCERS

LINE OF RETREAT

HASHEEN HILL

ROYAL ARTILLERY

GUARDS

DENSE BUSH

ARAB POSITIONS

17TH NATIVE INFANTRY

HASHEEN WELLS

15TH SIKHS

ROYAL 28TH NATIVE MARINES INFANTRY

HILLS OCCUPIED UNTIL RETREAT

LINE OF RETREAT OF AMARAS

BERKSHIRE REGIMENT

BENGAL LANCERS

47

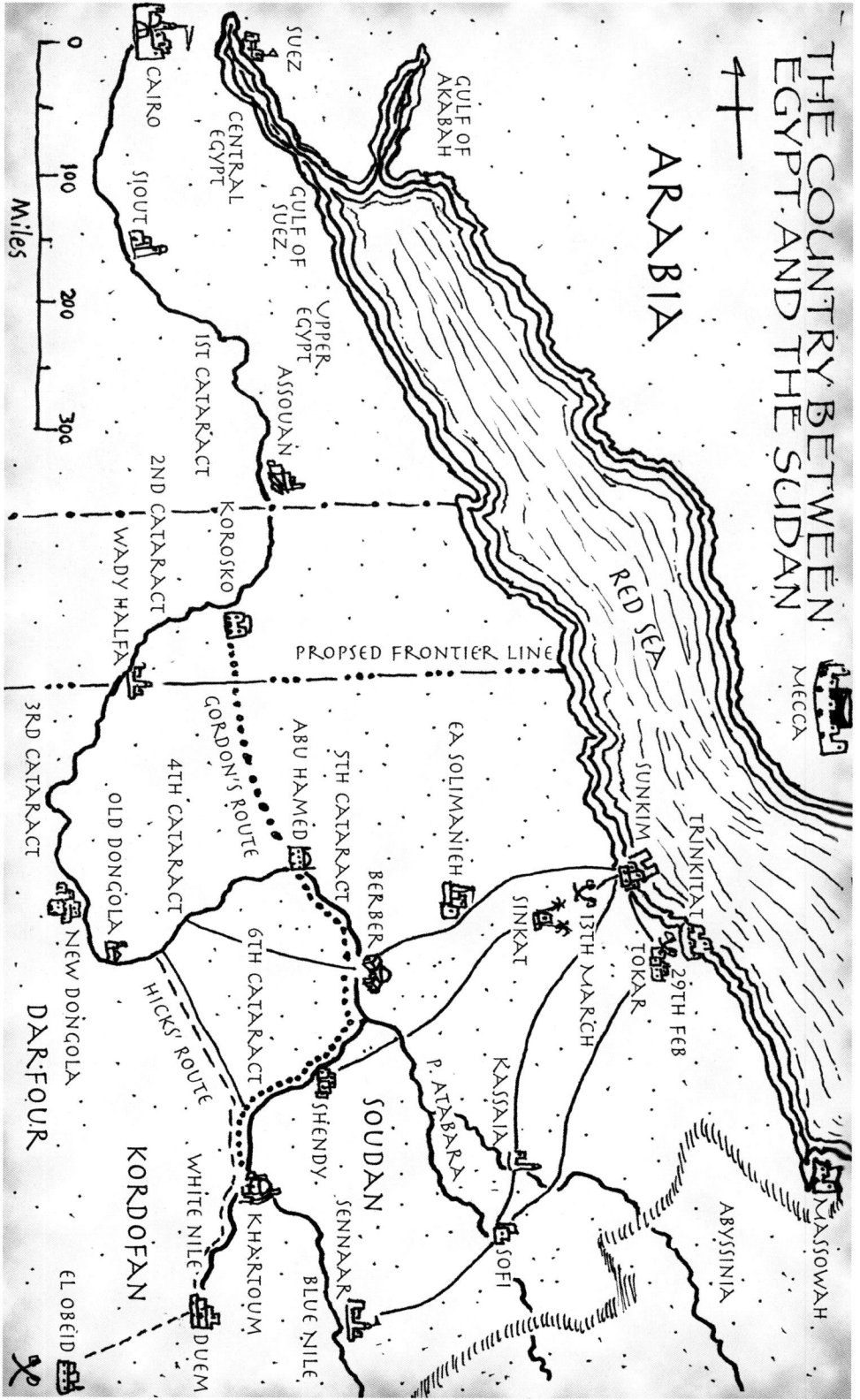

THE COUNTRY BETWEEN EGYPT AND THE SUDAN

ARABIA

0 100 200 300 Miles

CAIRO
SUEZ
GULF OF AKABAH
SIOUT
CENTRAL EGYPT
GULF OF SUEZ
UPPER EGYPT
ASSOUAN
1ST CATARACT
2ND CATARACT
KOROSKO
WADY HALFA
3RD CATARACT
RED SEA
MECCA

PROPSED FRONTIER LINE

GORDON'S ROUTE
ABU HAMED
5TH CATARACT
EA SOLIMANIEH
SUNKIM
TRINKITAT
13TH MARCH
SINKAT
TOKAR
29TH FEB
BERBER
4TH CATARACT
OLD DONGOLA
NEW DONGOLA
DARFOUR
HICKS' ROUTE
6TH CATARACT
SHENDY
SOUDAN
KASSALA
R. ATABARA
SOFI
ABYSSINIA
MASSOWAH
KORDOFAN
WHITE NILE
KHARTOUM
SENNAAR
BLUE NILE
DUEM
EL OBEID

48

A group of 5th Lancers from the Light Camel Regiment.

Tofrek 22nd March 1885

Feeling that his right (or west) flank was now more secure, General Graham set about establishing a forward base prior to his advance against Tamai, some 12 miles to the south west. Major General Sir John McNeill VC was tasked to construct and garrison two zarebas as an intermediate supply post in the desert. General McNeill was given two British infantry battalions (1/Princess Charlotte of Wales's [Berkshire Regiment] and Royal Marine Light Infantry), three Indian infantry battalions, two engineer companies and a naval detachment with four Gardner guns.

General McNeill's men moved in two large squares, preceded by a squadron of the 5th Lancers. The Indian battalion square encompassed the baggage animals (580 camels carrying 11,500 gallons of water; 500 supply camels; 400 pack mules; miscellaneous other pack animals) and made slow progress through unfriendly terrain.

General McNeill halted his men at Tofrek, about five miles south west of Suakin - short of his intended halt, but offering a chance to sort out the baggage train.

In a large clearing in an extensive belt of thorn scrub, three camps were established; a central, larger one for stores and two smaller ones either side for the British infantry who were to stay. The Indian infantry would be returning to Suakin.

As the work on the camps progressed, outlying pickets of the 5th Lancers reported Osman Digna with 5-8,000 men rapidly closing from the east, west and south. Driving the baggage animals and taking advantage of the confusion this caused, the tribesmen swarmed into the British positions.

Caught badly deployed, the British infantry sought to regain some semblance of order as they poured what fire they could into their attackers. The crews of the Gardner guns were cut down before they could bring their pieces into action and all over the battlefield, isolated groups of men stood their ground as best they could.

The bulk of the enemy's attack fell on the Berkshire battalion who gallantly stood their ground, supported by the 15th Sikh infantry.

British firepower and discipline gradually began to tell and as the troops organised a defensive position, the native attack faltered and stopped. General McNeill's command lost 117 officers and men in the action, with another 179 wounded or missing.

In the days following Tofrek, more stores were moved up and the position strengthened. The move on Tamai continued unopposed on 3rd April and the place was in British hands.

The projected Suakin-Berber railway began to take shape, protected by outposts and patrols formed from General Graham's command.

The Australian Contingent

Gordon's exploits were well known throughout the British Empire and when a telegraph brought word of his death to the New South Wales government, it offered a contingent of troops and to meet the expense involved. London accepted, but stipulated that the Australian contingent would be under British command. Similar offers from other Australian colonies and from Canada were declined.

The New South Wales contingent, an infantry battalion of 24 officers and 522 men, as well as an artillery battery of 212 men, anchored at Suakin on 29th March 1885 and was attached to a brigade under Major General Fremantle, composed of Coldstream and Scots Guards.

Guards Brigade (Major General Lyon Fremantle)
- 1 / Coldstream Guards (840)
- 2 / Scots Guards (840)
- 3 / Coldstream Guards (834)
- New South Wales Contingent (546)

They were issued with khaki uniforms and Martini-Henry rifles.

Shortly after their arrival they marched as part of a large 10,000 strong square to Tamai, a village some 30km inland. Although the march was marked by minor skirmishing, the Australians sustained only three casualties, none of which were fatal.

After this march the greater part of the contingent worked on the railway line that was being laid across the desert towards Berber.

When a camel corps was raised, 50 men volunteered. On 6th May 1885 they rode on a reconnaissance to Takdul but saw no action. Indeed, the camel corps only made one more sortie on 15th May, to bury the bodies of the men killed in the fighting at Hasheen the previous March.

When the British government decided to abandon the campaign the Australian contingent sailed for home on 17th May 1885.

The Sirdar and his staff welcomed into Berber.

The Background to 1896-1898

Conditions in Sudan had deteriorated under the rule of the Mahdi and continued to do so under Khalifa Abdullah el-Taaishi; economic and social chaos engulfed the country.

The Khalifa waged an incessant war against the Nile peoples of the south, adding large areas of territory to Egyptian Sudan and undertook various other military adventures, including an abortive attempt to conquer Egypt in 1889.

Egypt had by this time become a virtual possession of Great Britain. In 1896 the British and Egyptian governments, alarmed at the spread of French influence from west and central Africa into the Sudan, decided that it was necessary to re-occupy the Sudan as British, French and Belgian claims were converging on the country and it was feared that other countries with colonial aspirations could take advantage of Sudan's precarious situation to acquire territory. Further, control of the River Nile was seen as vital for purposes of transport, irrigation and security.

Accordingly a joint Anglo-Egyptian military expedition was sent against the Khalifa to re-conquer the Sudan.

The British Army 1896-1898

Organisation

Most of the British army infantry regiments were organised into two battalions; generally the 1st battalion served abroad while the 2nd battalion was deployed within the UK. This was not always strictly the case however and there were some 2nd battalions serving in the Sudan; 2/Lancashire Fusiliers and 2/Rifle Brigade are two examples of this.

The battalion were composed of eight 120 man companies. A company was further divided into two half-companies, commanded by subalterns, each consisting of two sections under sergeants. Drummers could still play their battalions into action, as did the drummers of The Lincolnshire Regiment at Atbara River. The drummers were also responsible for sounding field calls on the bugle. Their only armament was the 1895 Pattern drummer's sword.

Cavalry regiments were usually composed of four squadrons, each 160 strong. Each squadron had three or four troops, each of three or four sections, each of four two-man files.

Uniforms

The reconquest of the Sudan was the first campaign in which the new khaki drill uniform issued to the British army for all foreign service was universally worn. Yellowish buff or brown in colour, khaki blended in well with the colours of the terrain, be it on the North West Frontier of India or in the Sudan.

The khaki uniform had brown belts and white ammunition pouches. An oval pattern water bottle was carried.

The Rifle Brigade still maintained the British army's tradition of rifle regiments having black leather equipment, but the 1888 pattern however was to be the last equipment made in black.

The sun helmets had khaki covers with quilted neck curtains with regimental cotton badges and badges displayed on the left side. Officers of all arms tended to wear the new Wolseley helmet.

The 2nd Battalion The Rifle Brigade, who did not arrive in Sudan until August 1898 from Malta benefited from being equipped with blue sun veils and goggles.

The distinguishing marks worn on the side of the helmets of the battalions deployed to the Sudan were as follows:

The Cameron Highlanders	A blue square patch
The Grenadier Guards	A red and blue rosette
The Lancashire Fusiliers	A square yellow patch
The Lincolnshire Regiment	A square white patch
The Northumberland Fusiliers	A diagonal red band around the helmet
The Rifle Brigade	A dark green patch
The Seaforth Highlanders	A white plume
The Warwickshire Regiment	A red square patch

The two Highland battalions still retained their kilts, bringing some colour to the appearance of the infantry.

The infantry carried the Slade-Wallace equipment - or, more correctly perhaps, the Valise Equipment Pattern 1888. This consisted of a valise, two braces, a waist belt, two pouches, a mess tin and cover, a haversack, a water bottle and carrier, two coat straps, one mess tin straps, a frog for the bayonet and a second for an entrenching tool. The two main Orders of Dress for the equipment were Service Marching Order and Light Service Order, the difference being that the valise was not worn with the latter.

The only British cavalry regiment in the Sudan was the 21st Lancers and they were kitted out with the same regulation khaki tunic and helmets as their infantry comrades. On each shoulder were epaulettes on ring mail, a very last vestige of the armour the cavalryman had worn in days gone by. Fawn colour breeches of Bedford cord were reinforced with soft leather on the inside leg and the cavalry boots were black and fitted with steel spurs.

In addition, the troopers carried a 50 round ammunition bandolier over their left shoulders, a white haversack and water bottle over the right shoulder. The 21st Lancers at Omdurman were mounted, not on the powerful weight carrying troop horses they rode in England, but on wiry little Arabs that a horseman at home would perhaps class as big ponies.

The saddles were of the 1890 pattern and were well adorned with such items of kit as a pair of leather wallets, equipment rolled in a groundsheet, a sword in its scabbard, the lance with a red over white pennant, the Lee-Metford carbine, forage sack, rope, picketing peg and mess tin fixed to it.

Weapons

The infantry armed with the bolt action Lee-Metford rifle, fitted with a magazine containing eight rounds of ammunition and which gave almost twice the rate of fire of the Martini-Henry. The rifle fired a .303" calibre high velocity smokeless cordite bullet, the rate of fire was one round per 2½ seconds using the magazine, although the weapon could be used as single shot at 12 rounds per minute, keeping the magazine rounds for rapid fire in an emergency. The bayonet was the new pattern sword bayonet issued in 1888 and was 12" long.

The American invented Maxim machine gun was introduced into service with the British army in 1891 and gradually issued to the infantry and cavalry. It weighed 40lb and fired 650 rounds a minute.

The cavalry were equipped with Cavalry Sword Pattern '90 (ie 1890) - which was not popular with the troopers, for it was said to bend on impact and to be unbalanced - and the Lee-Metford carbine. The nine foot lance had a shaft of ash or bamboo and was tipped with steel point. Officers carried the Heavy Cavalry Pattern sword.

In 1894 a new 12pdr 6cwt breech loading gun was introduced to replace the previous 12pdr which had proved to be too heavy for the horse artillery and it was this gun, along with the 15pdr that was used in the Sudan. The pieces fired a new high explosive shell that had greater range and multi-splintered fragmentation.

Also in service were 5.5" howitzers firing lyddite, a new high explosive adopted for the bursting charge of common shell for all breech loaders and howitzers over 4.7" calibre.

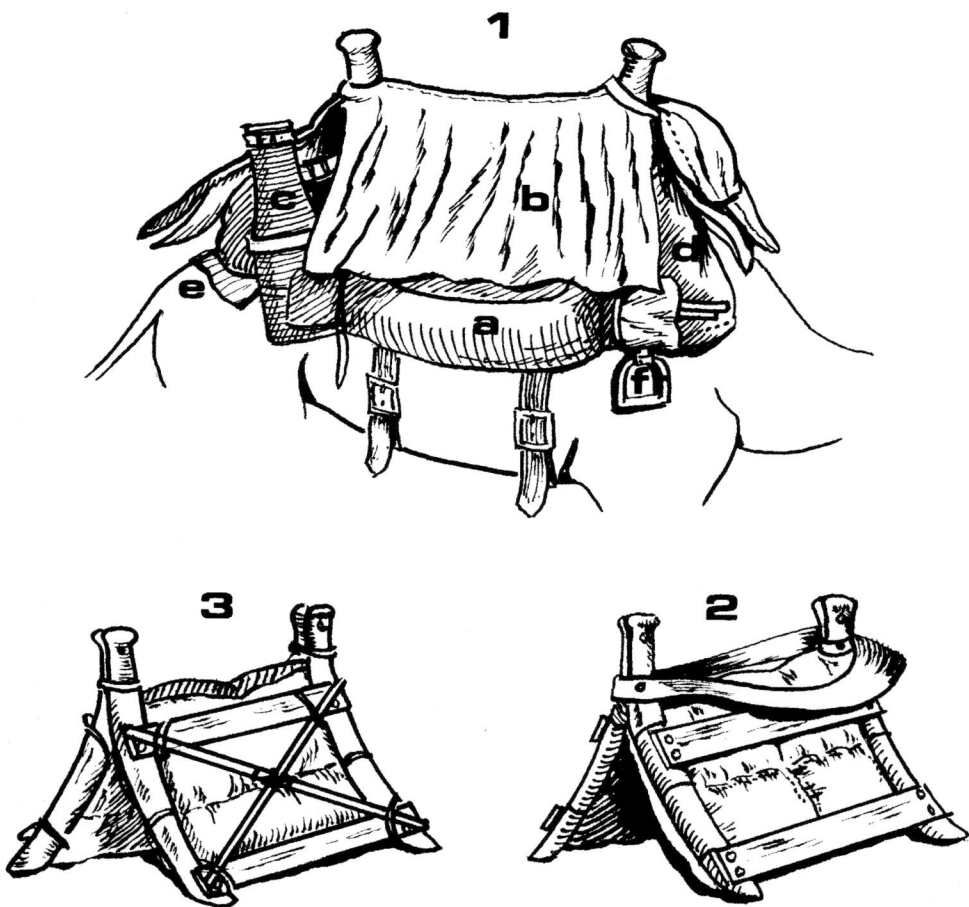

Drawings based on contemporary illustrations of the Mounted Infantry type saddle, and the 'knifeboard' or load bearing saddle for equipment etc.

Figure 1 Camel equipment (offside).

        a 'Zuleetah' of red leather and white canvas.

        b Saddle cover of red leather.

        c Namaqua rifle bucket of brown leather.

        d 15lb bag of corn.

        e Water skin of leather resting on a yellow leather flap.

The saddle was also festooned with a tent or tents, blanket roll and numerous leather cushions. A further long water container called a 'mussek' was also carried on the nearside opposite the rifle bucket. Also carried on the nearside was the greatcoat and waterproof sheet. The stirrups (f) were either nailed or hung around one of the wooden frames of the saddle.

Figure 2 The Mounted Infantry saddle without equipment.

Figure 3 The 'knifeboard' or load bearing saddle.

The load bearing 'knifeboard' baggage saddle.

The Camels

Two types of camel were used in the Sudan, the Arabian riding camel and the Egyptian baggage camel. The former could march five miles an hour for four or five hours at a time, but on longer journeys four miles an hour was the maximum that could be expected.

The pace of a baggage train was two and a half miles an hour and a loss of around 5% was expected when the animals could not be fed well.

The normal daily ration for each camel was 12lbs of beans and 15lbs of chopped sava grass. Camels carried some 400lbs exclusive of their saddle; this weighed 42lbs and the rest of the kit - feeding bag etc - another 70lbs.

The baggage train had around one camel for every two arms chests, four camels per troop or company for their general stores. A good quality baggage camel was expected to carry six boxes of rifle ammunition.

The Nile Gunboat Flotilla

General Kitchener fully appreciated that to have any chance of success he had to achieve full command of the Nile waters. His flotilla of river gunboats carried sufficient firepower - artillery, rapid firing weapons such as the Maxim and Nordenfelt, plus 6pdr guns and quick firing 12pdrs - to take on any enemy forts and enough armour plating to defend them against artillery fire.

When the *Zafir* blew up, Commander Kepple the flotilla commander transferred to the *Sultan*, one of the three new twin screw gunboats. (The others were *Sultan* and *Melik*)

The *Melik*, *Sheik* and *Sultan* were new twin screw gunboats. Built in London to Kitchener's specifications, the vessels were dis-assembled and shipped to Alexandria and Port Said, then transported by river and rail to Kosheh, south of Firket for re-assembly.

The *Melik* saves the Camel Corps from being slaughtered at Omdurman.

Trans-shipped seven times, the craft arrived without the loss of a single major piece and more than a fortnight early and that on a schedule of only eight weeks for construction.

The crews were a mixture of British, Egyptian and Sudanese service personnel and civilians of many nationalities. The gunboats were well equipped with weapons, manned by Royal Marines. Some of the vessels mounted powerful searchlights.

After the Omdurman campaign most of the gunboats entered service with the Egyptian army.

The gunboats were:

Zafir
- Commander C Keppel RN Flotilla Commander
*Abu Klea (*Stern paddle-wheel)
 - Captain Newcombe RN
El Hafir
- Lieutenant C M Staveley RN
Fatch
- Lieutenant Beatty RN
   (*Destined to find fame as commander of the British Battle Cruiser Squadrons at Jutland 1916.*)
Melik
- Major Gordon RE
Metemma
- Lieutenant Stephenson RN
Nazir
- Lieutenant the Hon A Hood RN
   (*This officer was to become an admiral and lost his life commanding the 3rd Battle Cruiser Squadron at Jutland 1916.*)
Tamai
- Lieutenant H F Talbot RN
Sheik
- Lieutenant Sparks RN
Sultan
- Lieutenant W H Cowan

Hadendowah ('fuzzy-wuzzy') warrior
(Artist: Bob Marrion © Bob Marrion 2007)

(L) Member of the Desert Column Guards Camel Regiment
(R) Grenadier Guard in khaki drill, Suakim Field Force

Naval Brigade, Sudan 1884-85. L-R: Lieutenant, Seaman, Lieutenant. (Artist: Bob Marrion © Bob Marrion 2007)

A driver of the Army Service Corps wearing Service Dress c1898.
(Artist: Bob Marrion © Bob Marrion 2007)

A spirited illustration showing the attack on the zareba at Tofrek, when the Dervishes broke through, scattering the baggage and followers.

The charge of the 21st Lancers at Omdurman, after a painting by Harry Payne.

The Charge of the 21st Lancers at Omdurman, April 8th, 1898 (E.Matthew Hale)

An Egyptian detachment negotiates with a mixed force of Mahdists containing Nubians, Kordofans and Arabs, here led by a Darfur warrior in medieval armour.

The Egyptian and Sudanese Forces 1896-1898

Organisation

The Turko-Egyptian army of Arabi had been badly beaten by General Wolseley's army at the battle of Tel-el-Kebir in 1882 and finally finished off in November 1883 by the forces of the Mahdi.

Under Major General Sir Evelyn Wood's leadership and training a new Egyptian army began that same year, initially 6,000 strong organised into eight infantry battalions, a regiment of cavalry and two batteries of artillery. By the end of 1885 there were nine infantry battalions (one Sudanese), eight troops of cavalry, four artillery batteries and three companies of camel corps. The following year four more infantry battalions were raised, two Egyptian and two Sudanese, The two Egyptian formations were later disbanded to save money, but by the end of 1888 had been replaced by Sudanese battalions and the camel corps had increased to four companies. By 1891 there were 14 battalions of infantry (the last six Sudanese), five cavalry squadrons; six batteries of artillery (including one of horse artillery) and the camel corps now had six companies. At Omdurman the army mustered 20,000 men with 140 white officers in 19 infantry battalions, 10 cavalry squadrons, a horse artillery battery and four field artillery batteries and a camel corps of eight companies. There was also a military school for young officers and non-combatant support services.

The Egyptians (*fellahin*) were taught self reliance and had complete faith in their British officers. After 1885 the Egyptian army became a potent force and bore the brunt of the action against the Dervishes. The bulk of the rank and file were indigenous Egyptians who were conscripted for a period of six years.

An Arab 'friendly' with a camel carrying the Mounted Infantry saddle. Note the rhinoceros hide shield slung from the saddle pommel.

Of the Egyptian battalions, 1st - 4th; 15th - 18th had three to four English officers, but the 5th to 8th were officered entirely by Egyptians.

Each Egyptian infantry battalion was initially divided into four companies (*buluks*), each of approximately 200 men, but in 1898 the battalions were expanded to six companies 100-120 strong, giving battalion strength of 650-750.

Sudanese blacks formed six infantry battalions, the 9th to 14th - although in fact Sudanese formations were given Roman numerals - from 1890 organised into six companies, each of some 150 men. The Sudanese formations were generally regarded as the cream of the army. These battalions were often positioned forward in the firing line with the Egyptian battalions in support.

The men in these units enlisted for life, but on a voluntary basis. These battalions had five British officers.

The camel corps operated in independent companies of about 150 men each. In total the camel corps was some 800 strong, half Sudanese, half Egyptian. They used the mounted infantry saddle, sitting astride. There were five white officers in the corps.

The Egyptian cavalry was initially organised into 70 strong troops, but from 1890 it was re-organised into squadrons of 100 men. The cavalry horses were stout, sturdy beasts of 13 hands or so, and they got through an amazing amount of work.

The artillery batteries had six guns each; machine gun batteries had two guns each.

Weapons

The rifle issued to the Egyptian and Sudanese infantry and the camel corps was the Martini-Henry black powder breech loader, a hard hitting and vicious weapon at close quarters. The rifle was fitted with a triangular socket bayonet.

From the 1890s the front rank of a cavalry squadron carried the lance as well as a sabre and the Martini-Henry carbine. Seven of the squadron leaders were English.

In the early 1880s the artillery used the 7pdr mountain gun, 9pdr and 14pdr Krupp breech loaders and 14pdr muzzle loading brass howitzers. When the British standardised the Egyptian army, the main field gun became the 6.5cm Krupp. From 1897, but by the time of Omdurman, all four batteries of field artillery are armed with Maxim-Nordenfeldt 75mm quick firer firing a 12½ lb shell or an 18pdr double shell, although No3 retained two of its Krupp pieces.

Multi-barrelled Gardner and Nordenfelt machine guns were used from 1896, Maxims from 1897.

The horse battery had some rather ancient 7.7cm Krupps. This piece suffered from a slow rate of fire and poor quality shells. The horse artillery guns were drawn by teams of six Syrian horses and ammunition wagons accompanied the guns into action.

Each artillery battery had a white commander and all the men were Egyptians.

Uniforms

The standard Egyptian uniform was khaki tunic and trousers, blue puttees, a red fez (*tarboosh*) with a short black tassel hanging from the top. Sudanese tassels could be black, green or red. The fez had a khaki cover and flap (*imma*) which hung down over the nape of the neck. The Sudanese troops did not require this protection and were issued with a plaited straw cover for the fez. Various flashes on the fez covers identified the different battalions.

General Hicks' Egyptian troops on their gruelling march to Kordofan
where they met their deaths.

Up to 1884 the Egyptian infantry wore a summer dress of white cotton cloth tunic and loose white trousers tucked into white gaiters, worn over black shoes. Winter dress consisted of a dark blue tunic with cream facings and dark blue trousers, the latter trimmed in cream. Equipment was black or brown.

From 1884 when on campaign, close fitting jerseys were worn, brown (or very dark khaki) for Egyptian troops, dark blue for the Sudanese. Sand coloured trousers with dark blue puttees, brown leather equipment and a white haversack completed the kit.

Officers wore the winter uniform of dark blue, in a French style; a single breasted, thigh length tunic with voluminous skirts, with baggy trousers tapered at the ankles.

The Egyptian cavalry's attire was a light blue uniform with white facings, but after 1882 the regular cavalry and camel corps wore khaki, although the Sudanese companies of the camel corps wore blue jerseys. The Egyptian artillery uniform was dark blue with scarlet facings, but khaki was worn in the same uniforms as those of the infantry.

Each infantry battalion carried a plain green silk flag (measuring approximately 100cm by 800cm) bearing the battalion's number in white Arabic numerals. Each company also had a small rectangular coloured flag bearing the company number and attached to a spear shaft and carried in front of the company on the march.

The Egyptian national flag was that of Turkey, red with a large white star and crescent in the centre.

The Dervishes 1896-1898

For comments on the organisation, uniforms and weapons of the Dervishes please see the relevant section in Part One of this present work.

The Re-conquest of the Sudan 1896-1898

In 1892 Major General Sir Horatio Herbert Kitchener (1850-1916) became *sirdar* or commander of the Egyptian army and started preparations for the re-conquest of the Sudan. The British government authorised General Kitchener to undertake a campaign with the intention of re-conquering the Sudan. Britain was to provide some of the troops and equipment, while Egypt was to finance the expedition as well as providing soldiers.

The campaign opened in mid-March 1896 with Egyptian soldiers moving up the River Nile and establishing a fortified camp at Akasha, located on the Nile approximately 80 miles south of Wadi Halfa, to provide a supply dump and cover for the construction of a military railway. General Kitchener planned every detail of the forthcoming campaign, and intended to use all means of transport to concentrate his army. Throughout April and May 1896 he consolidated his base at Akasha; the construction of the railway from Wadi Halfa continued and by the end of May, the line was 24 miles from his position.

A substantial forces of Dervishes under Utman al-Azraq began congregating at Firket, south of Akasha - and within a day's march - and established a fortified camp.

The Battle of Firket 7th June 1896

During the night of 6th/7th June General Kitchener ordered a force of 9,000 Egyptian and Sudanese troops to move by river and overland and attack the Dervish positions. A desert column of cavalry and camel corps under Burn-Murdoch marched inland to cut off the Dervish escape route, while the bulk of the force - 7,000 - under Hunter advanced up the Nile.

Macdonald's 2nd Brigade of Sudanese under attack.

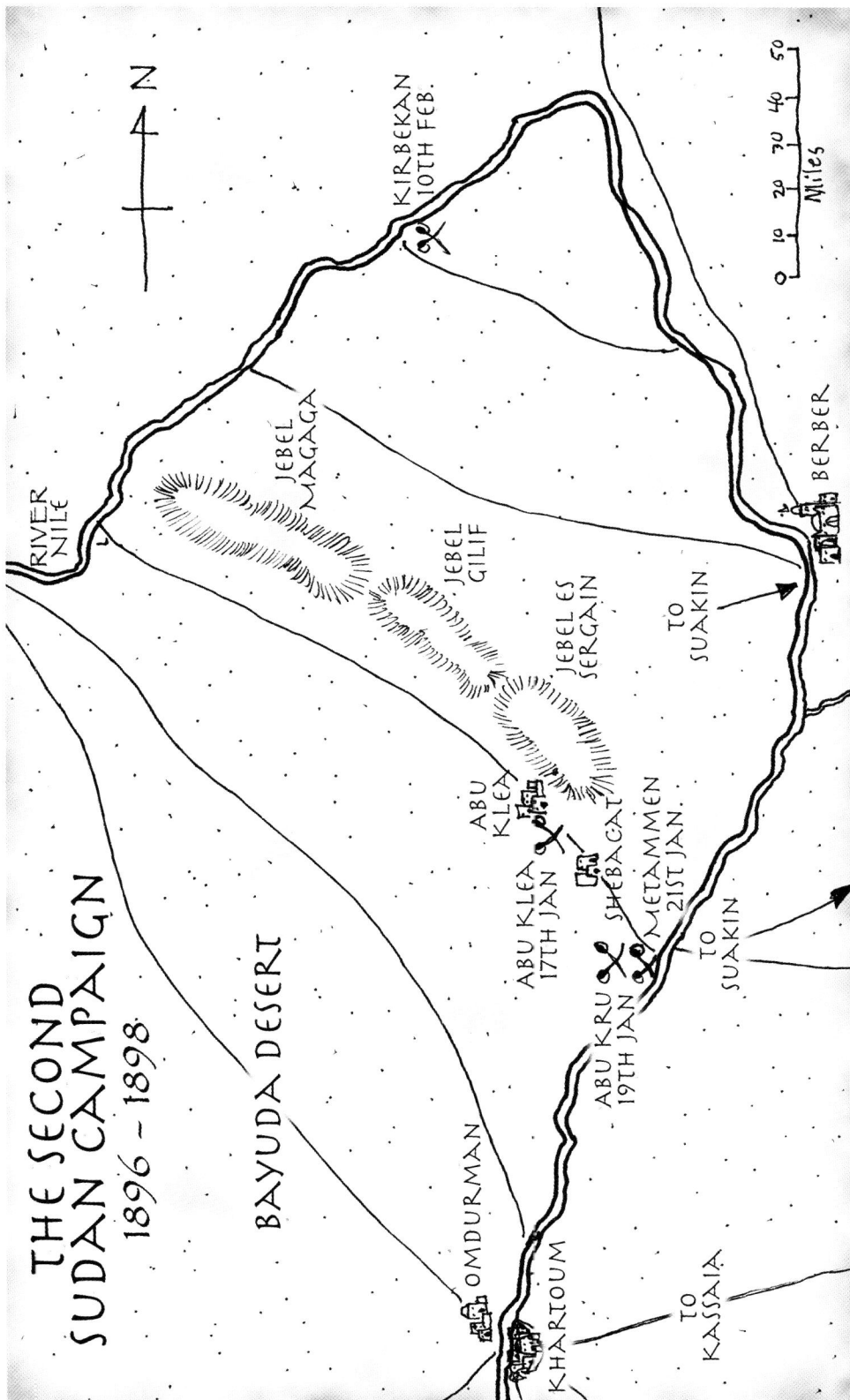

THE SECOND
SUDAN CAMPAIGN
1896 - 1898.

N

BAYUDA DESERT

RIVER NILE

JEBEL NAGAGA

JEBEL GILIF

JEBEL ES SERGAIN

KIRBEKAN
10TH FEB.

BERBER

TO SUAKIN

ABU KLEA

ABU KLEA
17TH JAN

SHEBACAT

METAMMEN
21ST JAN.

ABU KRU
19TH JAN

TO SUAKIN

OMDURMAN

KHARTOUM

TO KASSAIA

Miles
0 10 20 30 40 50

ATABARA CAMPAIGN
MARCH & APRIL 1898

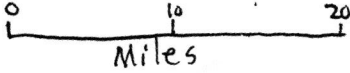

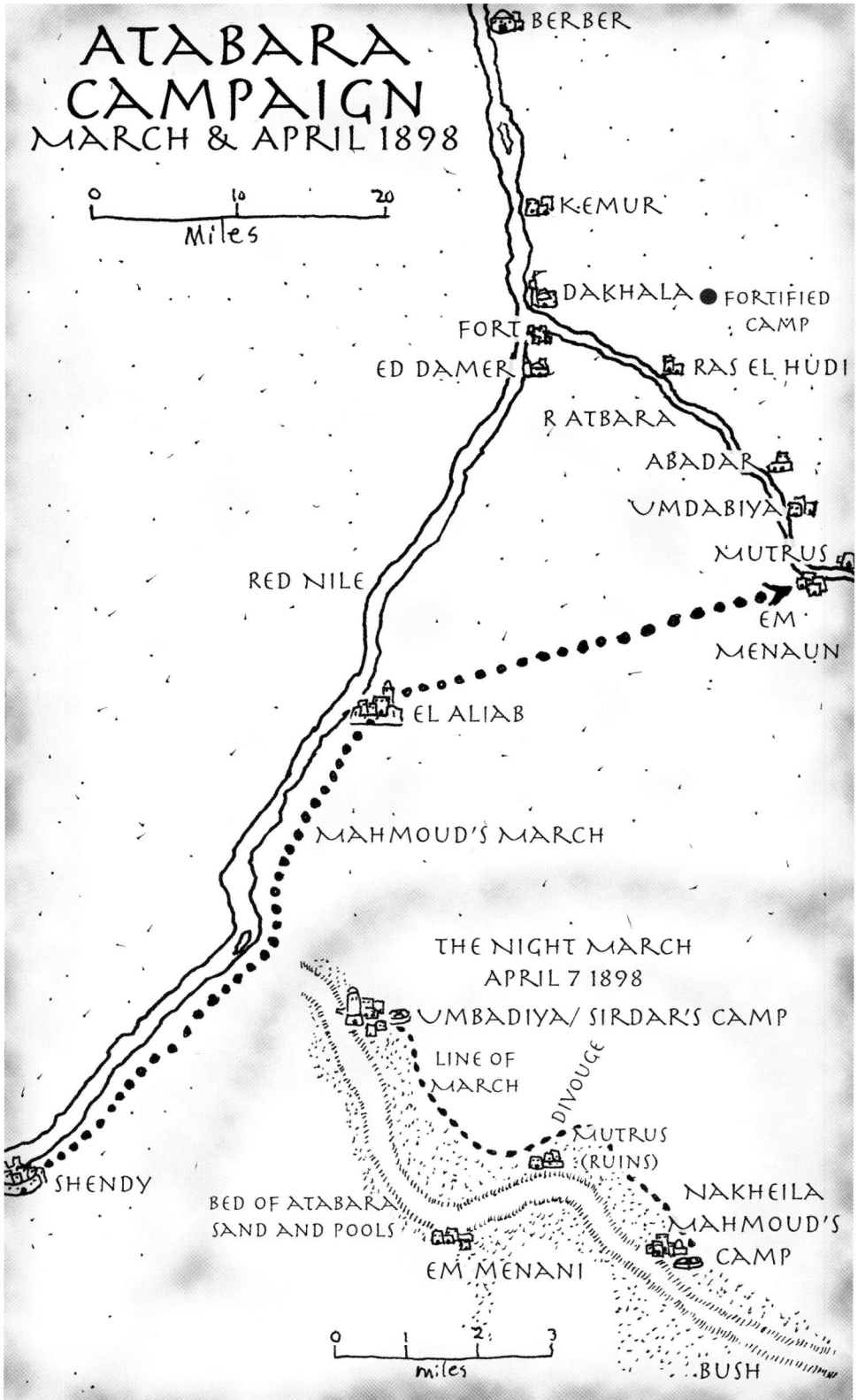

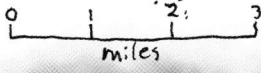

0   10   20
Miles

BERBER

KEMUR

DAKHALA   ● FORTIFIED CAMP

FORT

ED DAMER

RAS EL HUDI

R ATBARA

ABADAR

UMDABIYA

MUTRUS

EM MENAUN

RED NILE

EL ALIAB

MAHMOUD'S MARCH

THE NIGHT MARCH
APRIL 7 1898
UMBADIYA/ SIRDAR'S CAMP

LINE OF MARCH

DIVOUGE

MUTRUS (RUINS)

NAKHEILA
MAHMOUD'S CAMP

SHENDY

BED OF ATABARA
SAND AND POOLS

EM MENANI

0   1   2   3
miles

BUSH

Anglo-Egyptian Order of Battle at Firket 7th June 1896

The River Column (Hunter) 7,000

1st Brigade (Lewis)
- 3rd Egyptians
- 4th Egyptians
- 9th Sudanese
- 10th Sudanese

2nd Brigade (MacDonald)
- 11th Sudanese
- 12th Sudanese
- 13th Sudanese

3rd Brigade (Maxwell)
- 2nd Egyptians
- 7th Egyptians
- 8th Egyptians

4th Brigade (David)
- 1st Egyptians
- 5th Egyptians
- 15th Egyptians

- Also, four Maxim guns, manned by men of The North Staffordshire Regiment
- 2nd Egyptian Field Battery
- 3rd Egyptian Field Battery
- Two gun boats
- Three armed steamers

The Desert Column (Burn-Murdoch) 2,700

- Camel Corps, six companies
- Cavalry, eight squadrons
- 12th Sudanese (mounted on camels)
- Battery of Horse Artillery (6 x 6cm Krupp pieces)
- Two Maxim guns

In silence and with first class timing the troops carried out a surprise attack on the Dervish position and, after heavy fighting, completely routed the natives in an action that lasted for less than three hours. More than 1,000 natives were killed or wounded, with a further 600 being taken prisoner; Utman al-Azraq retreated southwards with the survivors. The Egyptian/Sudanese force lost 22 men killed and 91 wounded.

The battle is interesting, for it confirmed the fighting quality of the new Egyptian army, which was far superior to that of earlier conflicts.

The March to Dongola

After spending three months waiting for reinforcements and the arrival of a flotilla of gunboats, General Kitchener advanced southwards towards Dongola at the head of 13,000 men. As before, some of the troops marched overland, while some journeyed up the Nile in river steamers protected by the gunboats.

A Dervish force of 5,000 with six mountain guns under Muhammed-wad-Bushara had established an entrenched position at Hafir on the far bank of the Nile - the same side as Dongola, General Kitchener's objective.

General Kitchener ordered the artillery and gunboats to engage the Dervish lines, but this proved ineffective and eventually the gunboats moved past the Dervishes and on to Dongola.

The Dervish commander, wary of an attack against the rear of his position, abandoned Hafir and Dongola was taken without a fight. This success meant that over 450 miles of the River Nile had been secured against the Dervishes with minimal casualties.

The Dervishes retreated towards Metammeh, Berber and Atbara, all places to the south and in the general direction of Omdurman.

Action at Abu Hamed 7th August 1897

Work on a railway line from Wadi Halfa to Abu Hamed, south east across the Nubian Desert continued. A small Dervish force occupied Abu Hamed and in late July 1897 a flying column of 3,600 men (3rd Egyptians, IX, X, XI Sudanese, a field artillery battery, two Maxims and a troop of cavalry) under General Hunter set off to cover the 118 miles to the village, a feat achieved in just over seven days. Taken completely by surprise the Dervishes refused to surrender, so the Sudanese infantry were sent in with fixed bayonets. The natives fought hard, leaving 250 killed before being defeated.

Alarmed by the outcome at Abu Hamed, Zaki Uthman, the Dervish commander at Berber, over 100 miles away, fell back on Shendi, on the opposite bank of the Nile from Metammeh, and a further 100 or so miles away and south of the Atbara River. So it was that Berber, the most important strategic link between Wadi Halfa and Omdurman and situated north of the confluence of the Nile and Atbara Rivers, was occupied without a struggle.

The Atbara Campaign

Osman Digna, his position at Metammeh threatened by Egyptian forces at Berber and on the Red Sea coast at Suakin, moved south.

This meant that General Kitchener could use the old Suakin-Berber caravan route to assist his build up of supplies at Berber. He established a major fortified camp sited at the confluence of the Nile and Atbara Rivers and perhaps 20 miles south of Berber. In late October 1897 the railway reached Abu Hamed, which also made the maintenance of the Berber position that much easier.

In early January 1898 more British troops arrived in the Sudan via Cairo to Wadi Halfa. These were the first battalions of three infantry formations, namely The Royal Warwickshire Regiment, The Lincolnshire Regiment and The Cameron Highlanders from garrison duties in Egypt, with a fourth, the 1st Battalion Seaforth Highlanders, *en route* from Malta.

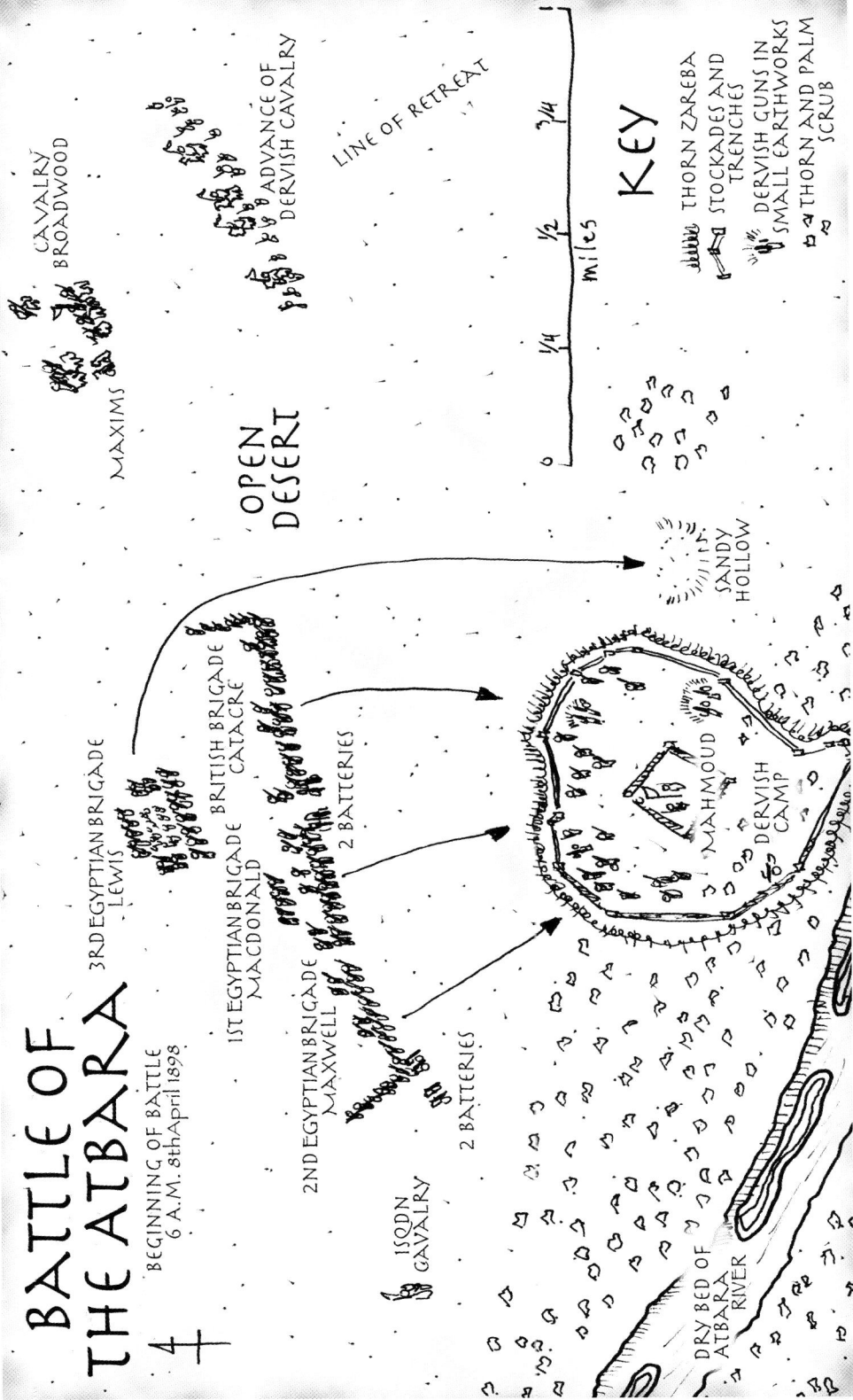

BATTLE OF THE ATBARA

BEGINNING OF BATTLE
6 A.M. 8th April 1898

CAVALRY
BROADWOOD

MAXIMS

ADVANCE OF
DERVISH CAVALRY

LINE OF RETREAT

OPEN DESERT

3RD EGYPTIAN BRIGADE
LEWIS

BRITISH BRIGADE
CATACRE

1ST EGYPTIAN BRIGADE
MACDONALD

2 BATTERIES

2ND EGYPTIAN BRIGADE
MAXWELL

2 BATTERIES

1 SQDN
CAVALRY

DRY BED OF
ATBARA
RIVER

SANDY
HOLLOW

MAHMOUD

DERVISH
CAMP

KEY

THORN ZAREBA

STOCKADES AND
TRENCHES

DERVISH GUNS IN
SMALL EARTHWORKS

THORN AND PALM
SCRUB

miles
0   ¼   ½   ¾

The Seaforth Highlanders storming the Dervish zareba at Atbara, after a painting by Caton Woodville.

By the end of the month an Egyptian army of three infantry brigades, eight cavalry squadrons and four artillery batteries held the River Nile from the fortified camp to Abu Hamed.

Initially the four British infantry battalions were stationed some 30 miles south of Abu Hamed, but when Emir Mahmud Ahmad - the Khalifa's cousin - and a 10,000 strong Dervish force arrived at Nakheila on the Atbara River south east of the fortified camp, they marched up to within 10 miles of the camp.

The Dervishes also established a camp with its rear resting on the Atbara River and surrounded by dense thickets of thorny bushes.

The Battle of Atbara River, 8th April 1898
When it became apparent that Mahmud Ahmad was not going to attack his position at Fort Atbara, General Kitchener reluctantly marched towards the Dervish position to give battle.

The general's army was the strongest and best equipped that had yet been seen following the Egyptian flag on the Upper Nile. In all there were some 12,000 men present in the field. An armed river flotilla escorted the army.

The infantry were divided into four brigades:

British Brigade - Brigadier General Gatacre
- 1/Cameron Highlanders
- 1/Seaforth Highlanders
- 1/Lincolnshire Regiment
- 1/Royal Warwickshire Regiment
- Plus six Maxim machine guns

Egyptian Infantry Division - General Archibald Hunter

1st Brigade - Brigadier General H MacDonald
- 2nd Egyptian
- 9th Sudanese
- X Sudanese
- XI Sudanese

2nd Brigade - Brigadier General Maxwell
- 8th Egyptian
- XII Sudanese
- XIII Sudanese
- XIV Sudanese

3rd Brigade - Brigadier General Lewis
- 3rd Egyptian
- 4th Egyptian
- 7th Egyptian

Cavalry - Colonel Broadwood
- Eight Egyptian squadrons
- A battery of Maxims on galloping carriages, with teams of mules
- Egyptian Camel Corps

The army marched out from the camp on 4th April and formed four brigade squares with General Gatacre's British Brigade leading, followed by General Hunter's Egyptian Division. The cavalry provided two squadrons to cover the army's advance; the rest of the mounted troops and the artillery were to follow some hours later and catch up with the infantry during the night.

After short halt about a mile and a half away from the Dervish camp during the night of 8th April, and at dawn, the troops deployed into a two deep line attack formation. Moving through scattered bush and scrub, the men reached the top of a ridge overlooking a shallow depression where, barely 600 yards away, lay the Dervish positions.

An undulating surface of sand and stones, with tufts of coarse, dry grass extended to the Dervish position and amid the palms and along the edges of the camp could be seen the Dervishes with banners flying. The great zareba hedge looked like a grey-green wall running through the scrub under the palms.

The enemy camp was about 1,200 yards across and sheltered from fire by rising ground, its rear resting on the Atbara River and surrounded by dense thickets of thorny bushes. The camp itself was surrounded by a zareba of desert thorn piled up and twisted together, so that in places it was 10 feet high and 20 feet across, inside this was a low stockade of palm tree logs and three lines of trenches. Behind these was a labyrinth of trenches, rifle pits, bomb proof shelters, mud huts and smaller straw constructions. Here and there in the camp were small earthwork forts containing one or two brass cannon and 40-50 Dervishes.

The Mahdist cavalry had mounted and were trotting out into the desert to the right, watched by Colonel Broadwood's squadrons

A heavy bombardment of shells and rockets opened up for an hour on the enemy camp to prepare the way for the assault. After the barrage stopped, General Kitchener gave the order to resume the advance. The zareba was reached and gaps were torn through it. The British infantry poured through the gaps, coming under heavy fire from Dervishes occupying the stockade and trench lines. Also, as already noted, concealed amongst the thick bush was a complicated network of foxholes and rifle pits and the earth seemingly erupted with Dervishes, running and firing as they fell back before the determined advance and firepower of General Kitchener's infantry. Each of the numerous earthworks dotted around the camp had to be attacked and stormed and in the centre, on a rising knoll of ground was a square enclosure defended with a trench and a hardwood stockade. Manned by some of the best Dervishes, this proved a tough nut to crack, but eventually the position was taken.

The British troops advanced across the zareba area to the rear positions and through thick undergrowth to the river beyond. Isolated pockets of Dervishes held out, refusing to surrender and each had to be overcome.

On reaching the banks of the Atbara River, the infantry fired volley after volley

AREA AROUND OMDURMAN 1898

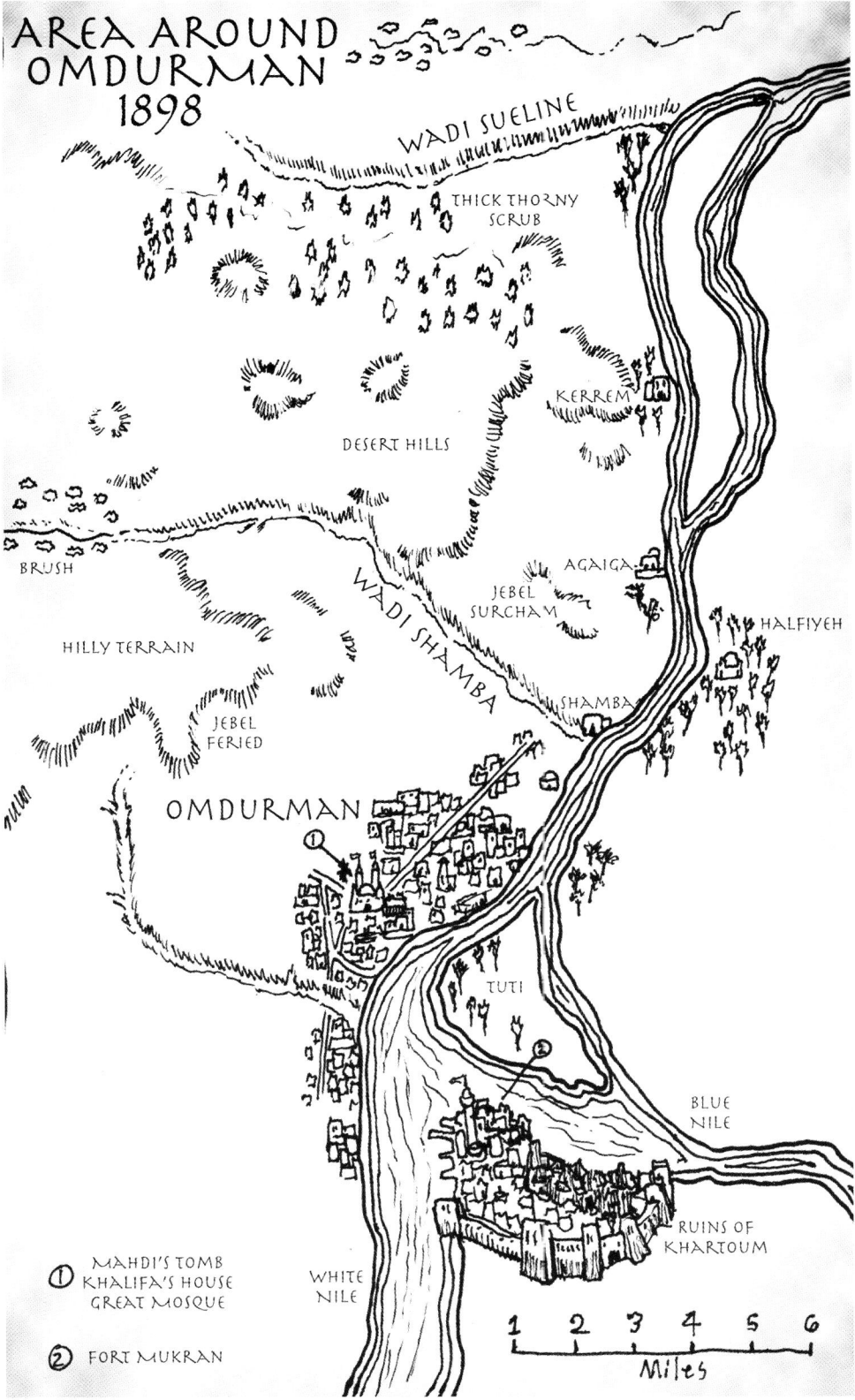

WADI SUELINE

THICK THORNY SCRUB

KERREM

DESERT HILLS

BRUSH

AGAIGA

WADI SHAMBA

JEBEL SURCHAM

HALFIYEH

HILLY TERRAIN

JEBEL FERIED

SHAMBA

OMDURMAN

①

TUTI

BLUE NILE

RUINS OF KHARTOUM

① MAHDI'S TOMB
KHALIFA'S HOUSE
GREAT MOSQUE

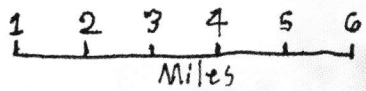

② FORT MUKRAN

WHITE NILE

| 1 | 2 | 3 | 4 | 5 | 6 |

Miles

across the virtually dry river at the fleeing Dervishes, inflicting heavy casualties. Colonel Blackwood's cavalry crossed the river and inflicted further losses on the fleeing natives.

The battle was over, but at some cost as the Anglo-Egyptian army sustained over 550 casualties, the British troops suffering 26 killed and 99 wounded.

Mahmud Ahmad's army was destroyed, with over 1,000 killed and many taken prisoner, including Mahmud Ahmad himself, captured in the central fort of the camp. The rest of his army scattered into the desert and ceased to be an effective part of the Khalifa's army.

The fight at Atbara had done much more than put an end to the Dervish advance on the Upper Nile; it had opened the way to Omdurman and Khartoum.

The Battle of Omdurman 2nd September 1898

By mid August 1898 General Kitchener was concentrated around the River Nile's Sixth Cataract, less than 50 miles from Omdurman.

His force had been strengthened by arrival of the 1/Grenadier Guards from Gibraltar, the 1/Northumberland Fusiliers and 2/Lancashire Fusiliers from Cairo, 2/Rifle Brigade from Malta and the 21st Lancers from Egypt, as well as some additional artillery. Thus he had around 22,000 troops, 44 guns, 20 Maxim machine guns and a fleet of gunboats, 10 of which were armoured.

The capture of the Emir Mahmoud - the Khalifa's cousin - leader of the Dervish army at the Atbara River, with troops of the X (10th) Sudanese Battalion of the Egyptian brigade.

Officers of the 21st Lancers whose regiment was attacked by the Dervishes at Omdurman.

The Anglo-British Army Order of Battle at Omdurman

General Kitchener commanding

(8,200 British, 17,600 Egyptian/Sudanese, on land 44 guns and 20 Maxims, on the Nile 36 guns and 24 Maxims)

British Infantry Division (Major General Sir William Gatacre)
- 1st Brigade (Wauchope)
- 1/Royal Warwickshire Regiment
- 1/Lincolnshire Regiment
- 1/Seaforth Highlanders
- 1/Cameron Highlanders
- Six Maxim guns manned by 16 Company, Eastern Division Royal Artillery
- Royal Engineer detachment
- 2nd Brigade (Lyttelton)
- 1/Grenadier Guards
- 1/Northumberland Fusiliers
- 2/Lancashire Fusiliers
- 2/Rifle Brigade
- Four Maxim guns manned by Royal Irish Fusiliers
- Royal Engineer detachment

Egyptian Division (Major General Archibald Hunter)
- 1st Brigade (Brigadier General Hector MacDonald)
- 2nd Egyptians
- 9th Sudanese
- X Sudanese
- XI Sudanese
- 2nd Brigade (Maxwell)

79

- 8th Egyptians
- XII Sudanese
- XIII Sudanese
- XIV Sudanese
- 3rd Brigade (Lewis)
- 3rd Egyptian
- 4th Egyptian
- 7th Egyptian
- 15th Egyptian
- 4th Brigade (Collinson)
- 1st Egyptian
- 5th Egyptian
- 17th Egyptian
- 18th Egyptian

Cavalry (Burn-Murdoch)
- 21st Lancers (4 Squadrons)
- Egyptian cavalry (9 Squadrons)
- Camel Corps (8 Companies)

Artillery (Long)
- 32nd Field Battery Royal Artillery (8 guns)
- 37th Field Battery Royal Artillery (6 x 5" howitzers)
- 1st Egyptian Horse Artillery Battery (6 x 6cm Krupp guns and two Maxims)
- 2nd Egyptian Field Battery (6 x Maxim-Nordenfelts, 2 x Maxims)
- 3rd Egyptian Field Battery (6 x Maxim-Nordenfelts, 2 x Maxims)
- 4th Egyptian Field Battery (6 x Maxim-Nordenfelts, 2 x Maxims)
- 5th Egyptian Field Battery (6 x Maxim-Nordenfelts, 2 x Maxims)

Naval Forces
- Three 1889 class armoured screw gunboats
  (Each 2 x Nordenfelt guns, 1 x 12pdr Quick Firer, 1 howitzer, 4 Maxim guns)
- Three 1896 armoured stern wheel gunboats
  (Each 1x12pdr Quick Firer, 2 x 6pdrs, 4 Maxim guns)
- Four old class armoured stern wheel gunboats
  (Each with 1 x 12pdr, 2 x Maxim-Nordenfelts)

On 24th August the march on Omdurman began and General Kitchener's army moved out in successive divisions, led by the cavalry and camel corps. These mounted troops were stationed well out to the right; the gunboats secured the River Nile and some Ja'alin friendly natives of the Arab Irregular Force under Major the Hon. E J Montagu Stuart-Wortley marched on the Nile's far (ie east) bank.

On 1st September 1898 the army formed camp in arc on a plain some 11km (6.5 miles) north of Omdurman around the village of Egeiga close to the bank of the River Nile, where a gunboat flotilla waited in support, facing a wide flat plain with hills rising to the left and right. A zareba was constructed around the camp and the British and Egyptian cavalry were stationed on the flanks.

Dervish cavalry charging.

The Dervish Army at Omdurman (c51,000)

Dark Green Flag (Muluazimayya) commanded by Uthman-al-Din
- 28,378 men, 2,925 mounted, 12,872 rifles and three artillery pieces
- (One 'French' gun, one mountain gun, one Remington machine gun)
- This force was made up of black Africans and Western Arabs, with no tribal levies.

Black Flag (Al-Rayya Al-Zarqa) commanded by Yaqub
- 14,128 men, 1,588 mounted, 1,053 rifles, two guns
- (One Krupp, one Nordenfelt)
- At Omdurman the Black Flag was composed of small tribal units, ranging from as few as 12 to as many as 1,600 men

Green Flag (Al-Rayya Al-Khadra) commanded by Khalifa Ali wad Ullu
- 5,394 men, 794 mounted.

Osman Digna (No flag, captured at Tamai 1884)
- 3,371 men, 187 mounted, 365 rifles

Red Flag (Al-Rayya Al-Hamra) commanded by Khalifa-al-Sharif
- 81 men

Amir Othman Azraq
- Personal bodyguard of 71 men

The Dervish army under the Khalifa numbered around 50,000 of which some 3,000 were cavalry. The army was split into five groups; a force of 8,000 under Azbak was arrayed directly opposite the British, the other forces were initially concealed. Abdullah al-Taashi and 17,000 men were hidden behind the Surgham hills to the west and rear of Azbak's force, 20,000 more were positioned to the north west close to the front behind the Kerreri Hills, commanded by Ali-Wad-Helu and Sheik ed-Din. A final group of 8,000 was gathered on the slope at the right flank of Azbak's force.

General Kitchener feared that the Dervishes would launch a night attack on the camp from the surrounding hills, so the troops slept with their rifles.

Just after 6:30 in the early morning of 2nd September the men in the camp could see the Dervishes advancing, and the first action began with a charge straight at the Anglo-Egyptian force by the 8,000 men under Azbak from the Dervish army. This was quickly followed by a further 8,000 from those waiting to the north west.

The British artillery (32nd Field Battery RA) opened fire at around 2,800 yards and the Dervishes were badly hit before they even came in range of the Maxim guns and rifles. This initial frontal attack in crescent mass continued and was directed principally at the British brigades; the infantry and Maxims on the Anglo-Egyptian left and front were heavily engaged and coming under long range fire from Dervishes on the slopes of Jebel Surgham to the Anglo-Egyptian left.

More of General Kitchener's artillery engaged the Dervishes and the Grenadier Guards began firing at 2,000 yards. As the natives came closer more and more of the infantry, standing in double rank behind their low zareba, opened fire.

The Dervishes continued their attack, dividing into masses of about 4,000, covering the entire area between the hills and the entire ridge from Jebel Surgham to the Nile.

Shortly after 8am the main attack was finally repulsed and the Dervishes retired behind the hills.

The 21st Lancers charge at Omdurman.

Officers of the 3rd Battalion, Grenadier Guards, Suakin 1885.

The Egyptian cavalry and camel corps in the Kerreri Hills to the right of the Anglo-Egyptian position were almost trapped by the advance of native elements attempting to move around General Kitchener's right flank, but were rescued with supporting fire from a gunboat on the River Nile, assisted by land based artillery.

The main Dervish force was kept at bay by gunfire from the zareba and the gunboats.

The general assumed the action was over and, anxious to occupy Omdurman before the remaining Dervishes could withdraw into the town, he ordered his troops to advance on Omdurman. The army was formed into brigade lines of parallel columns at such an interval that they could at once deploy into fighting formation and began to advance out from their zareba.

The 2nd British Brigade (Lyttelton's) led the way with its left on the river bank, its front facing south. Next to it, a little to its rear and right came Wauchope with the first brigade. Next and still further to the right came Maxwell's Brigade and then Lewis's. Thus the left of the leading brigade was covered by the river and the gunboats, while the next brigade covered its right flank and had its own landward flank covered by the next in succession.

MacDonald's Brigade marched well to the rear of Lewis's and was nearest to the hills. Between it and the river and further back came the camel corps and the Egyptian cavalry. Collinson's Brigade formed up close to the village to escort the transport train along the Nile bank and served as a reserve to the whole.

The 21st Lancers, with their four squadrons in line were sent ahead to clear the long slope that ran down from Jebel Surgham to the Nile, find out if any Dervishes had rallied and if so, cut them off from Omdurman. When the 350 strong regiment sighted a force of some 300 Dervishes on an apparently open plain, they charged,

The painting of the battle of Omdurman by R Talbot Kelly, representing Brigadier Hector Macdonald's Egyptian brigade repelling the attack by the forces of the Khalifa.

eager for action. Suddenly between them and the Dervishes there was a deep ravine beyond the slopes of Jebel Surgham filled with a solid mass of 3,000 - 4,000 natives. Too late to stop, the Lancers surged down the steep side of the ravine into the Dervishes. The cavalry went straight through and out the other side and were eager to charge back at the Dervishes, but the commanding officer Colonel Martin stayed their hand and ordered a number of troopers to dismount and open fire with their carbines at short range. The Dervishes, after firing a few shots in reply tried to retreat to the hills from the ravine that no longer protected them. As they did so, they were forced to cross in front of the British division who opened fire; only a small number of them reached the hills.

Sixty dead Dervishes were found in the ravine; the 21st Lancers lost five officers, 65 other ranks and 119 horses in the action, but gained three Victoria Crosses. (Awarded to Captain Paul A Kenna, Second Lieutenant Raymond H L J De Montmorency and Private Thomas Byrne.)

The British advance allowed the Khalifa to re-organise his forces and gather his army for one last effort. He still had more than 30,000 men in the field and directed his main reserve to attack from the west, while ordering the forces to the north west to attack simultaneously over the Kerreri Hills.

General Kitchener's force wheeled left in echelon to advance up Surgham ridge and then southwards to prevent the Dervishes retreating on Omdurman. To protect the army's rear, MacDonald's brigade of 3,000 Sudanese and Egyptians, re-enforced with Maxims and artillery was in reserve about a mile or two north of the main body.

A Camel Corps officer arrived at MacDonald's line and informed him that a flanking force of about 15,000-20,000 Dervishes from the west, out from behind Surgham, was moving towards his position.

84

MacDonald's men were all that stood between the main force and the oncoming Dervishes led by Yakub, the Khalifa's brother. General Kitchener was unaware of the danger and the army was marching in columns with their rear to the attacking Dervishes and ordered MacDonald to break camp and join the rest of the army.

MacDonald ignored the order, called in his four battalion commanders and quickly mapped out a plan of defence in the sand. He wheeled his men into line - the XI Sudanese on his left, the 2nd Egyptians in the centre, the X Sudanese on the right, with the IX Sudanese to the rear in support. Maxims were deployed on the flanks and batteries deployed between the battalions in gaps left for that purpose.

Meanwhile General Kitchener had been appraised of the situation by messengers sent by General Hunter was now aware of the grave danger the army was in and attempted to reverse his army and place the units back into fighting positions.

MacDonald's brigade met the attacking Dervishes with heavy fire, he kept his troops well organised and disciplined. When the second Dervish mass led by Osman Digna and Wad Helu appeared, charging from the Kerreri Hills on MacDonald's right, he swung back his right so that the IX and X Sudanese now faced northwards and poured their fire into this new attack.

The nearest infantry brigade was some distance away from MacDonald's men and for an anxious 10 minutes he had the battle all to himself.

The Dervishes nearly succeeded in closing to hand-to-hand combat with the brigade.

Help was to hand however. When General Kitchener saw the Dervish attack pouring down on his 1st Brigade, he sent the 32nd Field Battery to bring its guns to bear on Yakub's attack. Collison's brigade was set in motion towards MacDonald's right, and Lewis and Maxwell formed their brigades into line and marching on

The Anglo-Egyptian force advances towards Omdurman.

The aftermath of the 21st Lancers charge at Omdurman.

MacDonald's left, made for the rocky ground around Jebel Surgham from which Dervish riflemen and artillery were supporting the attack.

In response to a message from General Hunter, Wauchope's brigade was advancing at the double to form in MacDonald's rear. The gunboats added their firepower and shelled Osman Digna's division.

The Dervishes to the north had regrouped too late and entered the clash only after the force in the central valley had been routed. They pressed MacDonald's Sudanese formations hard, but they redeployed to meet the new direction of attack; the Lincolnshires came up and their sustained volleys repulsed the attack.

The British, Egyptian and Sudanese infantry fired volley after volley at their attackers and slowly the Dervish counter attack was driven back and the natives started retreating - a sight rarely seen on a Sudan battlefield.

A last desperate effort to save the day was made by the Dervish cavalry, but they were mown down by rifle fire.

The Dervishes were driven back on the Kerreri Hills and cleared from Jebel Surgham, fleeing westwards and thus leaving General Kitchener's route to Omdurman clear.

At the end of the five hour action, 10,000 Dervishes lay dead, 15,000-16,000 were wounded and 5,000 were prisoners. Kitchener's force lost four officers and 41 other ranks killed and 424 wounded, the majority from MacDonald's brigade.

The march on Omdurman was resumed at 11:30, many dispirited Dervishes could be seen plodding into the town, which was reached by General Kitchener's leading elements about an hour later.

On learning that a party of the Khalifa's riflemen were still occupying the walled enclosure near the Mahdi's tomb, the gunboats opened fire and the 32nd Battery dropped a salvo of shells at intervals in the same area, so as to make it untenable.

Guards were mounted on the principal buildings and the Khalifa's stores. Large amounts of ammunition, powder, some 60 guns of various types, plus vast quantities of rifles, swords, spears, banners, drums and other war material were captured on the battlefield or in Omdurman itself.

The Khalifa escaped a short time before the troops arrived in Omdurman and survived a half hearted pursuit by weary cavalry and camel corps.

General Kitchener was awarded the title Baron Kitchener of Khartoum for his victory.

The Battle of Umm Diwaykarat 24th November 1899

In the wake of Kitchener's victory at Omdurman, mopping up operations required several years. The Khalifa, Osman Digna and Shaikh al-Din and their remaining forces, still 25,000 strong, retreated southwards from Khartoum into the Kordofan region, which the Mahdists still controlled and where they managed to hold their ground for more than a year.

In October 1899 the British obtained information that the Khalifa and his forces were among his native Baqqara to the west of Kusti in Kordofan.

General Kitchener sent General F R Wingate with 8,000 men to intercept him.

General Wingate marched from Kusti to the mountains of Kordofan, destroyed a Mahdist supply unit and soon located the Khalifa's camp.

By this time the Khalifa's Sudanese forces still mustered around 10,000, The Khalifa decided to make a stand, rather than retreat further. During the night General Wingate approached the camp from the east and north. At about 5am on 24th November 1899 the Khalifa's men began to attack the approaching British, but were driven back by withering fire from the Maxim guns. The Khalifa's attempts to rally his men failed and he soon accepted that all was lost. He called his leaders to sit with him on prayer mats facing Mecca in the Muslim tradition - all were mown down by rifle fire.

The Mahdist losses were around 1,000, the British captured most of the remainder, including the Khalifa's son. Only Osman Digna escaped, to be captured a few weeks later.

The battle marked the end of Muhammad Ahmad's short lived Sudanese empire. The remnants of the Mahdists continued to resist for a short while under Omar Digba, but he was caught in January 1900.

Sudan's economy had been all but destroyed in the Khalifa's reign and the population had declined by about one half due to famine, disease, persecution and warfare. Tribes had been divided in their attitudes towards Mahdism, religious brotherhoods had been weakened and orthodox religious leaders had vanished.

On 19th January 1899 the British and Egyptian governments agreed joint sovereignty in the Sudan.

The charge of the Dervish forces at Omdurman.

The Dervish leader Osman Digna, a Hadendowah slave trader who supported the Mahdi from the start of the uprising and was present at both the Atbara and at Omdurman. He was finally betrayed by tribesmen at Tokar whilst trying to make good his escape.

Some War Gaming Considerations

Throughout this section, unless noted otherwise, the remarks can be taken to apply to both the 1884-1885 Gordon Relief Expedition and the 1896-1898 Re-conquest of the Sudan.

In this part of the book, the intention is to highlight various aspects of the Gordon Relief Expedition and the Re-conquest of the Sudan which war gamers might need to reflect in any rules that are used for table top actions.

The various points have been set out in alphabetical order, simply as a means of reference this arrangement is not meant to imply that any one particular point is more important than another.

After some comments on the particular point in question, some suggestions are offered pertaining to its war game relevance.

The section is rounded off by some very generalised comments regarding the availability of war game figures and rules.

Balancing Forces

From the actions recounted in the text, it will doubtless have been noted that all the numerical advantage was with the Dervishes - at Atbara for example, the natives had three men to every two of Kitchener's and moreover, they held a strongly entrenched camp. But the British generally had the overwhelming advantage given by superior armament, training and discipline. The strength of the armies cannot be gauged by merely counting heads.

One way to tackle the question of balance is to organise a British or Egyptian/Sudanese balanced force and work out some suitable opposition, or, raise a Dervish army and decide how strong the opposition needs to be for an interesting action. Whichever way round the problem is tackled, one thing is for sure, the war gamer is going to need a fair number of Dervishes.

Just how the war gamer arrives at the strength of the opposition to a created force is a moot point. Point values could be allocated at unit level or possibly applied to each individual figure and the two sides balanced in that manner, but how many points to allocate to a particular formation or individual?

The one aspect that continually comes across when reading about campaigns in Egypt and the Sudan is the superior firepower of the Anglo-Egyptian forces; such was the volume of small arms fire from the troops that the Dervishes were sometimes unable to close on them. On this basis, one might allocate an Anglo-Egyptian unit or figure say three times the points value of a Dervish unit or figure. Granted, should they be able to close, the Dervishes with their broad bladed spear, sword and shield, could give a good account of themselves, but they had to come into contact in order to do so.

This selection of a 3:1 ratio is fairly arbitrary, but it is based on experience and has worked well for my colonial games in the past; if the reader is unhappy with this, then try 4:1 or 5:1, but in truth one cannot go lower than 3:1 for anything like a balanced game.

The 3:1 ratio will work for purely infantry or cavalry/camel units, but specialised formations such as Maxim detachments or artillery batteries/sections need special

90

The naval brigade at El-Teb 28th February 1884.

treatment by being fairly heavily loaded. A Maxim equipped unit or an artillery formation should cost triple the points of an infantry battalion, which should eat in to the overall points total of an Anglo-Egyptian force.

One final comment; if a British infantry battalion of say 12 figures is given a value of 12 points, it is not fair to allocate just four points (at the suggested 3:1 ratio) to a Dervish unit that consists of say 50 or more figures. The two sides should have units of roughly the same size in order for the points differential to work. (See below for comments on unit sizes.)

Within the respective two sides, the balance between the three arms - infantry, cavalry and artillery - can be detected from the various orders of battle for the historical actions. As a rough guide, I tend to field four to eight infantry units (ie two brigades) for every one unit of mounted troops (cavalry or camels) and for each artillery/machine gun unit. This works well enough for the Anglo-Egyptians, but is a wee bit 'artillery heavy' for the Dervishes.

Within the 1896 Dervish strategical deployments (see below) a ratio of five infantry (taken in this context to mean natives armed with rifle or sword, as opposed to spears) to one cavalryman to 10 spearmen falls out. The small number of artillery pieces is completely lost in such an exercise. Granted there was a fair amount of artillery at Omdurman, but that was the main Dervish arsenal where the pieces were stored and unless the war gamer intends to re-enact a particular scenario that requires them to have some artillery - El Teb and Atbara spring to mind - the Dervish artillery arm could reasonably be ignored.

The vicious fighting at Abu-Klea 17th January 1885.

Alternatively, taking overall percentages within the 1896 Dervish strategical deployments as a guide; of the Dervish total strength of 104,525 (including, to make the exercise work, the artillery pieces), the infantry make up 32%, the cavalry 6.3%, spearmen 61% and the artillery 0.07%. Thus in a 100 strong Dervish army the war gamer could field a mounted emir in command, leading 32 sword or rifle armed infantry figures, six cavalry and 61 spear armed warriors on foot - but no artillery until the force is <u>much</u> larger.

All these comments refer to generalised forces; if you are not satisfied the results, or if you intend to re-create one particular action, then as mentioned earlier, study the actual historical orders of battle and see what sort of ratios come out.

Dervish Strategic Deployment

In his excellent book *Omdurman 1898: Kitchener's Victory in the Sudan* (Osprey 1993) Donald Featherstone lists the Dervish dispositions in April 1896 as noted in the British Army's contemporary Sudan Intelligence Reports. As such information might be found most useful for a campaign, it is summarised here.

Location	Infantry	Cavalry	Spearmen	Guns
In Anglo-Egyptian Sudan				
Abu Hamed	400	100	700	4
Adarama	450	350	1,000	-
Berber	1,000	500	1,300	6
Dongola	2,400	500	5,000	8
Firket	250	100	1,000	-
Kardofan	6,000	350	2,500	4
Omdurman	15,000*	3,500	45,000	46
Upper Blue Nile	50	-	200	-
In the Dervish Empire				
Galabat	4,500	600	1,000	4
Gedaref	1,000	200	500	-
Kassala	900	400	1,400	-
Lado	1,800	-	4,500	3

(* figure includes 11,000 bodyguard)

Dervish Tactics

The Dervish tactics frequently disconcerted the British. The sound of the incessant drums produced the effect that the natives were miles away, but then they could rise from the ground a few yards away from a British position.

Running and then lying down in long grass or taking full advantage of the terrain features, such as depressions in the ground, was a favoured approach tactic, but once the battle lines closed, the sheer firepower of the well disciplined Anglo-Egyptian forces kept the natives at a distance.

The packed Dervish formations provided easy targets for British firepower, but some tribesmen with half a dozen wounds or so still kept going - some even regaining their feet after being hit and continuing to run.

Dervishes moved in great numbers, usually headed by a mounted Emir, with a standard bearer and attendants. They jogged forward, keeping time with the drum beats and covering ground at several times the pace possible by British infantry and at times matching the speed of galloping horses.

The two main factors in Dervish assaults were surprise and shock, often based on encirclement and attacks from more than one direction and often with overwhelming numbers.

Incessant sniping at the British whether in camp or on the march was a feature of the Dervishes and their riflemen also acted as skirmishers, often screening the main attack.

When faced with British cavalry, the Dervishes lay on their backs on the ground, where the troopers' swords could not reach them and attempted to hamstring the horses as they galloped past. Even the use of the lance was not successful in preventing this tactic.

The native attacks usually faded away as quickly as they had started.

Well disciplined, fearless and fast moving, the Dervishes were troublesome opponents for the British.

Earthworks

The Dervishes frequently made temporary use of naturally occurring earthwork defences, or hollows which could be deepened by being scraped out.

At the onset of the action at Atbara River 1898, the British infantry saw the Dervish position surrounded by a zareba. Inside the zareba were a low stockade of palm tree logs and three lines of trenches. Behind these was a labyrinth of trenches, rifle pits, bomb proof shelters, mud huts and smaller straw constructions. Here and there in the camp were small earthwork forts containing one or two brass cannon and 40-50 Dervishes.

Generally speaking such earthworks would be temporary, probably not particularly substantial and intended for concealment rather than for any defensive benefit.

It is quite difficult to represent a ravine on the war games table - although some ready made terrain squares can provide suitable, if necessarily shallow, features. The best approach might be for the Dervish player to either advise the umpire - if there is one - or to mark the locations of their forces on a map of the table top and for the figures to 'emerge' from a terrain feature as the Anglo-Egyptian forces approach. Not completely satisfactory perhaps, but even 6mm figures cannot really be concealed on the war games table.

When it comes to earthworks, then suitable terrain items intended for use in WW2 scenarios can be used quite successfully as artillery positions. With rifle pits, trenches and the like, the problem of concealment arises once more, so it is suggested that the same method as offered for the use of ravines or similar features is once more called into use.

River Boats, River Transport

In 1884 the British used the river steamers that belonged to the tourist operator Thomas Cook and Sons to move their men and supplies on the River Nile as far as Wadi Halfa. Some of these towed specially built 30 feet long whaling boats, but once a cataract was reached the steam boats were of no further use. Once this occurred it was sheer muscle power that moved the boats of the Gordon Relief Expedition up the Nile.

Gordon had seven armoured river steamers, some of which were fitted with small brass guns, and he sent four of them out from Khartoum to meet the relief force.

The Dervishes had two river steamers, the *Ismailia* and *al-Safia*, each armed with a mountain gun, plus one of the steamers (the *Bordein*) sent out by Gordon, captured, raised and refitted.

In his 1896-1989 Sudan campaign General Kitchener made good use of his flotilla of river gunboats. Such vessels were equipped with a variety of firepower from machine guns to quick firing artillery pieces, as well as armour plating to defend them against artillery fire. These were the *Abu Klea* (stern paddle-wheeler), *El Hafir*, *Fatch*, *Melik*, *Metemma*, *Nazir*, *Sheik*, *Sultan*, *Tamai* and *Zafir*. The *Melik*, *Sheik* and *Sultan* were new twin screw gunboats.

Some rather splendid models of gun boats are commercially available, certainly for 6mm, 25mm and 54mm figures, but these tend to be rather expensive. Alternatively, to scratch build a suitable vessel is not as daunting as it seems. There are two main considerations to bear in mind when beginning such a project; your model needs sufficient open spaces to allow figures to be stood on it and forget accurate scale. A model of a gunboat for war game purposes needs to be effective rather than decorative and various measurements need to be reduced to something practical for use on the table top, but still conveys 'the look of the thing'.

The very best source I have ever come across for information on building boats for colonial war games is contained within an internet website; Major General Tremorden Rederring's Colonial-era Wargames Page (http://zeitcom.com/majgen). This not only features beautifully illustrated battle/war game reports, there are pictures of war game figures, buildings, scenery, various types of ships and boats and

The gunboats fire upon the Dervishes *en-route* to Omdurman

so on. There are also details on how to construct a war game model of a native dhow - I urge you to view this website if you can. If I might use one quote from the text - *'Be ruthless with your ship sizes. The ironclad is 9" long, the gunboat 7½" and the steam launch 6". We know a steam launch is not two thirds the size of an ironclad, but we live with the discrepancy in order to place a reasonable number of figures on the launch and also keep the ironclad playable'*.

Sickness

Many of the casualties in the British forces were caused by the intense sun and the continuously high day time temperatures. Between May 1884 and February 1885, one infantry battalion alone lost 1,400 as a result of epidemics and a Royal Marine battalion had half of its strength sick at one time. The main causes were dysentery, enteric fever, typhoid and various other fevers. The heat, the lack of fresh food and water, and the generally unhealthy atmosphere all contributed to the troops' illnesses. Add to this the slow progress and presence of thousands of pack animals; camels, horses and mules and a somewhat unhealthy picture emerges.

Supply

Little attention seems to have been paid to logistical arrangements in the 1884 Nile Campaign. It appears that General Wolseley did not appreciate the need for a co-ordinated control of supply and transport by Commissariat and Transport staff. Even before leaving England he declared his intention of taking the control of the transport out of the hands of the Chief Commissariat officer and an infantry officer was appointed Director of Transport. Further, Wolseley decided that the Chief Commissariat officer should be attached to the staff of the general commanding the lines of communication (General Evelyn Wood), rather than to his own headquarters staff.

The Desert Column was dependent on pack animals, some 8,000 of which had been purchased, 2,000 less than the Commissariat had said were required. Just two Commissariat and Transport Corps companies (9 and 11) were deployed at cadre strength to supervise native camel drivers. The privates of these two companies proved impatient and unintelligent in their treatment of the natives and more trained officers were essential. The Director of Transport tried to compensate by using inexperienced regimental officers, whose mismanagement caused the loss of a great number of transport camels.

The relief of Khartoum failed in its objective, but it is worth noting that the final last hope dash across the desert to reach Gordon was delayed for eight days because there were insufficient camels to convey the essential supplies in one journey.

(See *Wait for the Wagon: The Story of the Royal Corps of Transport and its Predecessors 1794-1993*, Edited by Brigadier D J Sutton OBE and published by Leo Cooper 1998.)

The second expedition against Osman Digna, which operated out of Suakin in 1885 was supported by four companies of the Commissariat and Transport Corps. These companies, again at little more than cadre strength, operated a total of over 1,000 mules and 8,000 camels, all led by native drivers.

At Tofrek, where the Dervishes penetrated the British square, 12 men of the Corps were killed, together with 700 transport camels.

General Kitchener solved the problem of supply as his men advanced southwards by taking advantage of river transport supplemented by camels and by extending the railway as he progressed.

The problem for the war gamer here is two fold. Firstly, model transport camels are just as expensive as those of 'fighting' camels, even when the same figure/man (or, in this case perhaps that should be figure/animal) ratio as that used for the troops is brought into play. Secondly, such aspects as supply are considered deadly dull and not proper to the toy soldier world. Both are fair comment and supply problems really only come into play in a campaign scenario.

The maintenance of supplies is a difficult subject, whatever the period setting of the war game campaign and requires both research and paperwork. Once an initial supply figure has been established, the monthly, weekly or daily rate of consumption needs to be considered per man, per animal or per war game model - remembering that a ratio of perhaps one figure representing 50 men is being used. This applies to ammunition, food, water, animal fodder and so on. The ammunition stock will depend on the number of actions fought, but the remainder will decrease on a daily basis, even if the army simply stands still for a week.

In its simplest form, the question of supply needs such information as what is stored at your main base - and where is that base - and in what quantities, how large is the force being supplied, is there a railway, how many transport animals are available, what can they carry - and bear in mind that these themselves will need feeding - what is the daily consumption of all the carried commodities etc.

Such questions can really impact on the campaign abilities of an army and begin to touch on the continuing problems that had to be considered by 'real' generals in the field.

A view of the Sirdar's forces advancing at Atbara

Temperature

Whilst the desert and the areas in which most of the campaigning took place were generally very hot and very dry by day, at night the temperature could drop below freezing. It was frequently necessary for the men to don extra clothing at night and the officers habitually wore overcoats.

Seasonal variations are sharply defined in desert zones, where winter temperatures as low as 4.4 degrees C (40 degrees F) are common, particularly after sunset. Summer temperatures often exceed 43.3 degrees C (110 degrees F) in the desert zones and rainfall is negligible.

In the area around Suakin to the south of the Nubian Desert, the temperature averaged 125 degrees in the shade to 160 in the sun. Soldiers' lips cracked, festered and became swollen. To afford a degree of protection beards and moustaches were allowed and the men's' hair was cropped short.

Dust storms or *haboobs* frequently occurred in the hot summer months.

Terrain

The first general point that should be noted is that Sudan is a big country, the largest in Africa, with an area of more than 2.5 million square kilometres. The area can be roughly split into three natural regions; desert in the north, covering some 30% of the country, giving way to a vast semi-arid region of steppes and low mountains in central Sudan and finally the southern region of vast swamps and rain forest.

Most of the country comprises a flat, featureless plain. The Libyan Desert, a barren waste broken by rugged uplands, covers most of the Sudan north west of the River Nile. The Nubian Desert lies in the region to the east of the Nile and the Atbara Rivers. The latter waterflow is the most important tributary of the Nile. The few uplands include the Red Sea Hills along the coast and the Nuba Mountains in the west central area.

The Sudan's most important geographical feature and its life line is the River Nile. One of the longest rivers in the world, the 4,000 miles plus of the Nile follows a winding course throughout the length of the country. The river's two headstreams, the Blue Nile and the White Nile join at the capital and largest city, Khartoum. Between this point and its delta on the Egyptian Mediterranean coast the river has six all but impassable cataracts or steeply descending waterfalls between Egypt and Khartoum.

The main areas of cultivable land are situated in the region between the Blue Nile and the Atbara River, as well as the area between the Blue and White Nile in the centre of Sudan.

The country has vast areas of grasslands and forests. The southern part of the Sudan is scrub jungle and swamp land; the northern part is very dry and consists mostly of scrub desert with rocky outcrops and wadis, with large areas of shoulder high sava grass. The trees are mostly the thorny acacia and mimosa, which in some areas grow in thick clumps and in some number. Large forested areas are found in central Sudan, especially along the river valleys. Ebony trees are common in the valley of the Blue Nile, while ebony, mahogany and other varieties of hardwood trees are found in the basin of the White Nile.

The effect of the trees should not be over looked. During the march from Abu Klea in 1885 the British column became hopelessly lost in a thick wood of acacia trees. The baggage animals became entangled in the spiny trees and bushes and the soldiers were harassed, scratched and tired.

A year earlier the Desert Column was reported as having moved through rocky hills, low hilly country, open areas covered in gravel with an abundance of acacia and mimosa trees and large areas covered with tall sava grass. Equally, the terrain could be open and undulating with a few scattered trees.

Other species of indigenous vegetation include cotton, papyrus, castor oil plants and rubber plants.

The terrain around Suakin, the home of Osman Digna, featured contained shallow lagoons and marshes which were tidal and full of black mud impregnated with filth and refuse of every kind. Every time the tide receded this mess was left exposed to the glaring sun.

Scenery aimed entirely at the colonial war gamer is not too prolific, but many general items can be readily pressed into service. Palm trees intended to decorate the island hopping campaigns in the South Pacific during WW2 for instance can serve equally well in Egypt and the Sudan without raising too many eyebrows. With a few minor adjustments, a village pond can be adapted to represent an oasis; boulders and rocks are universal and box-like native dwellings are fairly simple to knock up. Garden centres are good sources of 'eastern' buildings, pyramids or vaguely palm like foliage - all items actually intended to adorn fish tanks.

Trains and Railways

Railways played an important role in the British strategy in the Sudan. In addition to being used to move troops and supplies, in the Gordon Relief Expedition improvised armoured trains were also used aggressively, as well as for night time reconnaissance of enemy positions. Tank locomotives were used as the motive power and these were protected by iron bars (the boiler), iron plates (the pistons and the driver's cab) and sand bags (the driver's cab). Positioned in front of the engine was a flat bed truck, typically mounting a 40pdr Armstrong gun in position, protected by steel plate. The first truck behind the engine had wooden 'kneeling height' walls, backed by iron plates and sand bags. The next or second truck carried two machine guns, a Gatling and a Nordenfeldt. Sometimes two further wagons were included, each carrying a muzzle loading 9pdr howitzer that could be off-loaded for use in field actions. Another specialised truck that was used provided an observation tower which was around 20 feet high. The train was manned by 50-60 Royal Marines and Royal Navy personnel and was usually crewed by Royal Engineers.

A second train supported the armoured train. This was fitted with a steam crane and carried ammunition, along with a selection of specialised stores and tools.

When it came to the Re-conquest of the Sudan, the railway line that was constructed across the Nubian Desert from Wadi Halfa - just south of the Egypt-Sudan border - to Berber, a distance of well over 300 miles, was intended as an important supply route. Berber was the end of the east-west caravan route inland from the port of Suakin, so also having a north-south railway line terminating at the town was a most useful contribution to the build up of supplies.

The war gamer is not particularly well supplied commercially with suitable trains.

Some are available in 6mm size and there are a couple (and these are really intended for the American Civil War) in 25mm, but there aren't many. There are some plastic kits available depicting items of WW2 vintage, but in actual fact, these are not too useful as they depict purpose built elements of armoured trains that were used during the war, typically in Russia. War gamers using 20mm or 25mm figures are however well supplied by the model railway fraternity, as a trip to your local model/hobby or toy shop will quickly reveal.

Assuming that all the original rolling stock etc. was shipped out to Egypt/Sudan from England, then the war gamer can quite happily use models of British railway equipment, be they engines or goods wagons of various types. A point in passing; 00 gauge equates to 1/72 scale, HO to 1/87 scale (or 4mm to the foot). There is also N gauge which at 1/160 scale or 2mm to the foot is roughly half the size of the 00 gauge.

Equally, since you're not a focussed collector of trains, a visit to a local toy fair to look for second hand items to mix and match can be a very effective and money saving outing.

A length of track - and it's useful to know that a couple of manufacturers (Hornby and PECO) offer yard/metre long lengths of continuous flexible track - laid down or across the table can really add to the period appearance of the colonial war games table. Mind you, it is important not to let the tail wag the dog and keep your railway involvement to a minimum; otherwise a whole new hobby starts to open up, and it's a slippery slope…

Wherever you happen to be though, it's worth keeping an eye out for railway items. Recently I found a train set quite by chance in a local 'cheapo' store for £2.99 - ideal for use with 15mm to (smallish) 20mm figures and I fondly recall a plastic '0' gauge train set I purchased in Calais for under £10. Both of these sets are/were American-ish in appearance, but 'painted down' and suitable weathered, they fitted the bill very well. They were also battery powered, but we war gamers don't want that do we? Do we? It's best to pretend not to see the 'looks' one receives from the women in your life - in my case a wife and two married daughters - when you explain just why you really do need this toy train set…

Airfix, now Dapol, produce fairly inexpensive 1/72 scale plastic kits of railway engines, rolling stock and accessories. These are excellent if you're OK with model making, but they serve really just as static models, I for one have never been able to make the engine's wheels move freely.

OK so we have a railway presence of some sort, what's to be done with it? Firstly, there is the scenic value. A war games table set out for a game and including a few bits of track, some points, some buffers and a rudimentary station look really good and offers the definite statement that this is not a Napoleonic battle on a sandy cloth.

Equally, just a simple length of track laid across, down or diagonally over the table sets off and identifies the period very well.

A number of real or imaginary scenarios involving the track and/or train spring to mind.

The train has to move from top left corner of the table top to bottom right as it is carrying much needed troops/ammunition/stores/water etc. A horde of natives wishing to prevent this from being achieved emerge from hiding firing their rifles and perhaps bringing some light artillery into play.

A town is being evacuated; civilians and their belongings, animals (why not?), stores and military personnel are loaded on to the train that sets off - only to find the line blocked by rocks placed on the track by tribesmen. The soldiers leap off the train to clear the rocks, only to find themselves under attack from waiting Dervishes.

Thus far the trains have been essentially civilian in nature; now add a couple of machine guns to open good trucks, or perhaps a field gun to a flat bed truck, place sandbags at strategic points and suddenly an armoured train enters play. This can operate in conjunction with the infantry and cavalry and support their attack on an enemy position.

A station complex of sorts was mentioned above; this could well come under attack from raiding natives, eagerly seeking plunder, food or whatever.

These are just a few of the possibilities that trains can bring to the war games table.

Unit Sizes
The first step is to establish a figure to man ratio. This might well depend on the rules that are going to be used, or tailored to the war gamer s need and available resources.

Anglo-British Units
The British infantry battalion in the Sudan had eight 120 man companies, giving a battalion strength of 960. British cavalry regiments consisted of four squadrons, each 160 strong, giving a regimental strength of 640.

Each Egyptian infantry battalion was initially divided into four companies, each of approximately 200 men, but in 1898 the battalions were expanded to six companies 100-120 strong, giving battalion strength of 650-750. We could conceivably amalgamate these two figures into an average of 800, but the options for both eras are quoted.

Sudanese battalions from 1890 were organised into six companies, each 150 men, totalling 900.

The Egyptian camel corps was around 800 strong and operated in independent companies of about 150 men each. The Egyptian cavalry was initially organised into 70 strong troops, but from 1890 it was re-organised into six squadrons of 100 men.

Using these strengths and adopting a preferred figure to man ratio - perhaps 1:33, 1:50 or 1:100 for example, the results, rounded off where necessary (I have a dreadfully tidy mind) might look something like this:

Unit and original strength		At 1:33 ratio	At 1:50 ratio	At 1:100 ratio
British infantry battalion	960	29 figures	19 figures	10 figures
British cavalry regiment	640	19 figures	13 figures	6 figures
Egyptian infantry battalion	800	24 figures	16 figures	8 figures
Egyptian cavalry regiment	600	18 figures	12 figures	6 figures
Egyptian camel corps	800	24 figures	16 figures	8 figures
Sudanese infantry battalion	900	27 figures	18 figures	9 figures

Whichever ratio is chosen - and it doesn't necessarily have to be one of the three suggested above - it is of paramount importance that the war gamer is consistent in the application of that ratio. So, it can be seen that the figure/man ratio is a very importance decision, bearing in mind that it must be applied across the board -

Dervish prisoners.

literally. A 29 figure strong British infantry battalion might look great on the table, but bear in mind that a (possibly) 10,000 strong Dervish army would require just over 300 figures to be represented at the same ratio. If you have the time, space and inclination, then go for it; if not you might consider the 1:100 ratio as a better alternative.

Much will depend on the size of the chosen figures; 6mm look very good '*en masse*', 25mm metal figures are not cheap, so there's a cost factor with a 19 figure cavalry regiment for example. For my own games I have used 6mm at the 1:33 ratio, then I moved over to gaming with 54mm toy figures in metal and plastic at the 1:100 ratio. Interestingly, when I passed on my 54mm colonial armies when we moved out of London, I subsequently went for 20mm figures, but still using the unit sizes that I had adopted in the toy soldier years. They were so familiar to me and seem to work, plus such units fit in very well into the much more limited space that is now available.

Dervish Units

The Dervishes are slightly more difficult to organise into 'units' as we understand them, but to briefly summarise the information from the earlier chapter on the Mahdist forces; the army was divided into a number of corps or 'flags'. Within the flags the natives were further divided into units of between 800-1,200 men. These were further divided into three fighting formations of spearmen, sub-divided into 'standards' made up of tribes or sections of tribes, then riflemen and the cavalry unit. Each 'standard' was further sub-divided into 'hundreds'. Further sub-divisions of 100 men within these units would be commanded by local sheiks, while smaller sections of perhaps 25 were also led by local sheiks. Outside this organisation were spearmen and swordsmen in tribal levy units, organised into separate commands in differing provinces.

Looking at this, let us propose that a 'flag' has say 4,000 warriors, which could be made up of four smaller units of 1,000 each. Each of these units would consist of spearmen, riflemen and cavalry - as there were more spearmen/swordsmen than any other type, shall we say a 500 for the spearmen and 250 each for the rifles and cavalry element for ease of reference? The unit of spearmen can be further sub-divided into 'standards' , then 'hundreds' and then finally sub-sub-units of around 25 men.

In a much generalised tabular form:

Unit and original strength		At 1:33 ratio	At 1:50 ratio	At 1:100 ratio
'Flag'	4,000	120	80	40
Smaller units	1,000	30	20	10
Spear sub-unit	500	15	10	5
Rifle/cavalry sub-unit	250	8	5	2
Spear 'standard'	250	8	5	2
Spear 'hundred'	100	3	2	1
Smallest unit	25	-	-	-

Now, it must be emphasised that this just a very generalised typical organisation, presented merely as a much generalised reference point. There were many variables even within the main army, and bear in mind that at the first level of sub-division of the 'flags', the units could be anywhere between 800 and 1,200 strong. Equally, there were units operating outside this system and others could be temporarily attached to a 'flag' as required.

Smaller Units

Another approach might be to operate at a much lower level, perhaps at company or squadron strength. British infantry companies in the Sudan were 120 men strong; Egyptian companies were either approximately 200 men, or 100-120 strong after 1898. Sudanese companies had 150 men, the Egyptian camel corps companies mustered about 150 men each.

British cavalry squadrons were 160 troopers strong, the Egyptian cavalry was initially organised into 70 strong troops, but from 1890 it was re-organised into squadrons of 100 men.

Thus the war gamer has smaller units to consider - 120-150 men for the infantry, 100-160 for the cavalry. Different figure/man ratios could therefore be used; 1:10 for example, giving unit strengths of 12-15 and 10-16 respectively. The Dervishes could be tackled in a similar manner; taking a 250 strong 'standard' of spearmen as an isolated example, then 25 figures would needed to represent the unit using the same ratio. War gaming at this lower level of organisation lends itself to skirmish war gaming wherein each figure takes on an individual persona and can be slightly wounded, promoted or awarded a medal or whatever as befits the occasion. Great fun!

Artillery

Thus far, I not mentioned the artillery (and for ease of reference I include machine guns here) in the discussion. As an ex-gunner, this pains me to say, but artillery batteries really can confound any selected figure to man ratio. With - at the most - six or eight guns in a full battery, and often being deployed in two-gun sections, any ratio is tested to the full. One approach is to consider the personnel rather than the pieces. Generally, a Royal Artillery field battery of six guns needed 200 men to operate, a Royal Horse Artillery battery, similarly of six pieces required 182 and a mountain battery 284. (The latter were not predominant in Egypt and the Sudan, but they were there.) Using the three ratios trialled above, these strengths come out at:

Unit and original strength		At 1:33 ratio	At 1:50 ratio	At 1:100 ratio
Field battery	200	6	4	2
Horse battery	182	6	3	2
Mountain battery	284	9	5	3

Machine guns tended to be manned by detached infantrymen or ratings from the Naval Brigade, but for each of reference, we can group these with a horse artillery battery, ie around 180 men. The resultant strengths can be used as a guide to the number of war game figures required to crew the battery, which is represented by one model piece. Each figure can represent one actual gun at 1:33 - and 1:50 at a pinch - and three guns using the 1:100 ratio. Not a perfect solution perhaps, but one which does provide the opportunity to include some artillery or machine guns in a force, whatever the chosen figure to man ratio. In all probability the rules to be used for the conduct of the war game will stipulate something along the lines of 'one gun represents six actual pieces' and this can also work well enough. Mind you, with one model on the table top depicting a full battery, detaching sections or sub-sections will not be easy!

The Dervish artillery can be treated in much the same manner, but bear in mind that overall the native artillery pieces were fewer in number and that any 'battery' organisation would be much more *ad hoc*. Unless the Dervishes are occupying a static position, allow a couple of field guns at the most and for field - ie mobile actions - it is probably best to ignore their artillery presence altogether.

Water

The need for water and a regular supply of the same shaped the course of the campaigns. The British could not move without a guaranteed supply and this predetermined what routes could be used. The importance of the River Nile and wells as sources of water cannot be stressed too highly. The Desert Column was forced to move from one water well to another as the men crossed inhospitable terrain. Sometimes the wells were good and the water plentiful, while on other occasions they were either drying up or could not support the numbers of men and animals that needed water.

During the second expedition against Osman Digna in 1885, one of the major problems was the distribution of drinking water. Sea water was distilled in condenser ships in the Red Sea off Suakin, then carried to the expeditionary force by hundreds of camels.

Zarebas

Zarebas (or zaribas) were temporary defences built by both the British and the Dervishes to encircle their camp sites. Some of the camels were made to kneel to form the shape required, then they were haltered by means of a loop of rope around their

The scene inside the zareba after the battle at Atbara River.

front legs. Their saddles and loads were then placed between four and six feet away to form an outer perimeter and thorn scrub was cut and placed on top of this barricade, up to a height of three or four feet to make a strong defensive wall. Wounded soldiers, stores, any remaining camels or mules and tents were placed in the centre whilst the infantry manned the defences, with machine guns being situated at suitable points. Sometimes temporary redoubts were constructed from boxes or camel saddles in addition to the zareba, or as 'stand alone' defences.

Often, the zarebas were merely meant as overnight affairs, designed purely to protect an army encamped before the march was continued the following day, but some could be quite substantial. At the onset of the action at Atbara River 1898, the Dervish position was surrounded by a great zareba of desert thorn piled up and twisted together, so that in places it was 10 feet high and 20 feet across, looked like a grey-green wall running through the scrub under the palms.

The simplest way to re-create a zareba for war game purposes is to use that familiar standby, lichen. This can be laid out in a most realistic fashion and benefits from the fact that the attackers or indeed the defenders can 'tear' gaps in the zareba to facilitate movement. Also, lichen can now be purchased in a number of shades, so the war gamer does not have to put up with a bright green hedge that is supposed to be representing desert thorn.

In war game terms, the zareba is a considerable obstacle to an attack, but provides no protection whatsoever from rifle or artillery fire.

War Game Figures

It is a certainty that any attempt to produce an 'up to date' list of manufacturers producing colonial figures in whatever size is doomed to dating and/or failure. New companies appear, older companies sometimes disappear, existing companies decide to add colonial figures to their existing ranges and on it goes...

Accordingly, I would simply suggest that would-be colonial war gamers keep an eye on manufacturer's advertisements in the hobby magazines, have a look at their websites and have a good look around at the next show you attend. The figures are there, from 6mm upwards.

War Game Rules

Much the same applies to the availability of rule sets suitable for colonial games. A quick check reveals over 20 sets currently available (2007), with perhaps twice that number being available via the internet. Not all of these specifically cover the 1884-1898 periods, but many of them do.

There is always the option of writing one's own rules for a given period, or even for a specific period. These can be as simplistic or complex as required; I have always found this to be a most stimulating and rewarding pastime - and no, I don't always win as a result of using my own rules.

Actions as War Games

The Battle of El Teb, 29th February 1884
(The First Expedition Against Osman Digna 1884)

An Outline of the Action

Osman Digna was a lieutenant of the Mahdi who had appointed him Emir of the Eastern Sudan. Digna's first act of aggression was to lay siege to Sinkat, some 60 miles from Suakin.

The Red Sea port of Suakin was important to the British - and Digna was well aware of this.

Initially the port was secured by Royal Marines from a naval squadron anchored off shore, and then more troops arrived from Cairo to form a stronger garrison.

On 23rd February 1884 Major General Sir Gerald Graham VC was given command of an expedition to both relieve Sinkat and defeat Osman Digna. Six days later he marched out at the head of some 4,000 troops, towards El Teb, where it was understood that 10,000-12,000 rebels were encamped.

General Graham's Approach March

General Graham's men approached the enemy position formed into one large square; in front were the Gordon Highlanders, in the rear the Black Watch, on the right the Royal Irish Fusilier supported by four companies of the King's Royal Rifle Corps and on the left the York and Lancaster Regiment, supported by 380 men of the Royal Marine Light Infantry. On the march the front and rear faces of the square moved in company column of fours, at company intervals, while the flanking formations moved in open column of companies. Intervals were left at the angles of the square for the guns and machine guns, the Naval Brigade occupying the front, the Royal Artillery the rear angles. The men marched with their water bottles filled and carrying one day's rations. The only transport animals were those carrying ammunition and surgical supplies, all being kept together in the centre of the formation.

The front and left of the square was covered by a squadron of the 10th Hussars, the right by a troop of the 19th Hussars, with the main force of the cavalry being in the rear under Brigadier Stewart.

The Dervishes Are Sighted

The natives fell back before the advancing square and at one stage all that could be seen were their various banners. The square changed direction and moved off to the right, halting frequently with the men adopting fighting positions, ie the four faces of the square facing outwards in order to quickly meet any assault.

After a period of eerie silence, Dervishes were sighted a few hundred yards from the square; these tribesmen fired their muskets and two Krupp artillery pieces also opened fire on General Graham's men. The square halted and the men were ordered to lie down as the field pieces and machine guns were brought into action. The Dervish artillery was silenced.

As the advance resumed, the square came under renewed musket fire and began to suffer casualties, but there was still no contact, as the Dervishes fired and retreated.

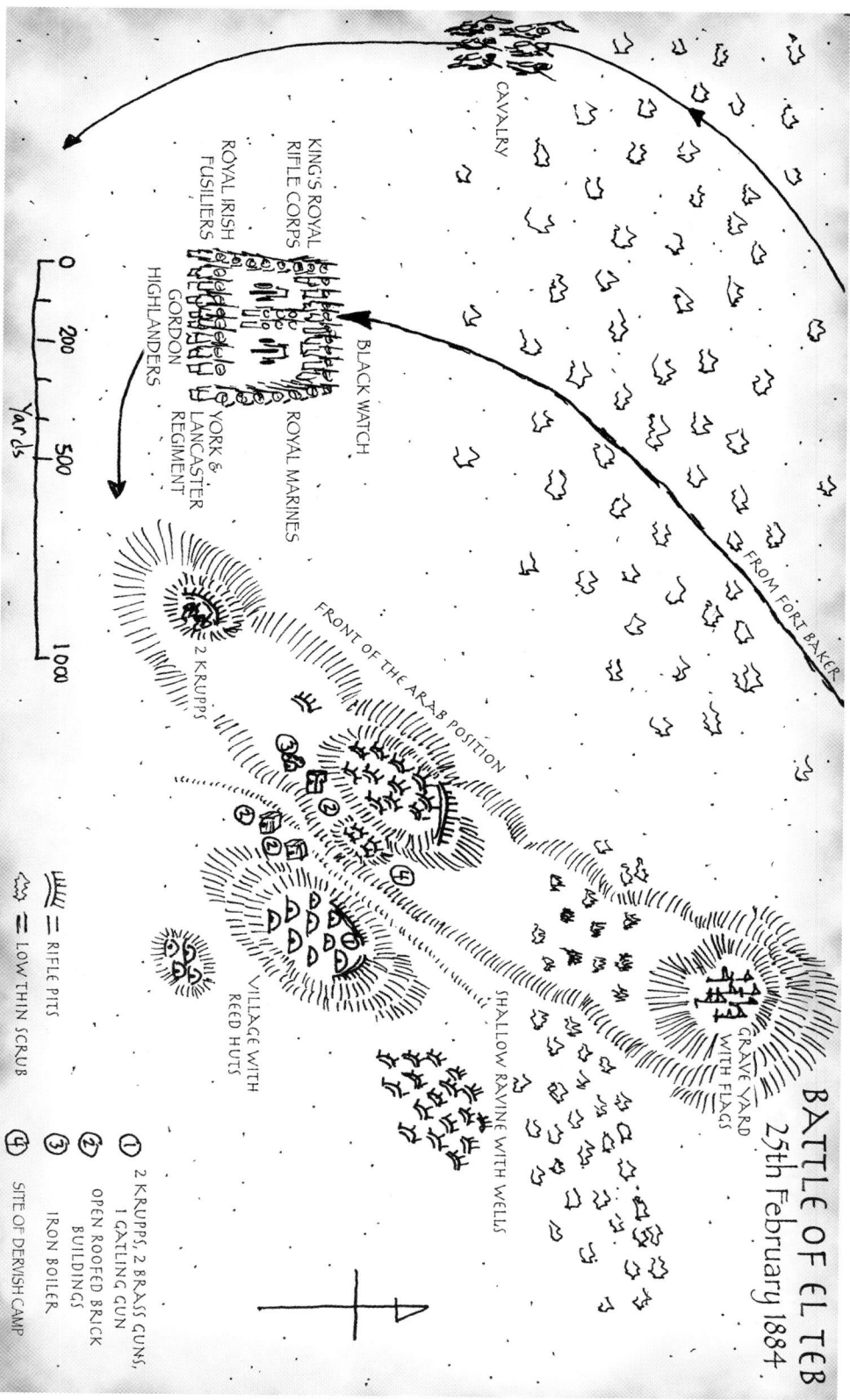

BATTLE OF EL TEB
25th February 1884

CAVALRY

KING'S ROYAL
RIFLE CORPS
ROYAL IRISH
FUSILIERS
GORDON
HIGHLANDERS
ROYAL MARINES
YORK &
LANCASTER
REGIMENT

BLACK WATCH

0
200
500
Yards
1000

FROM FORT BAKER

GRAVE YARD
WITH FLAGS

FRONT OF THE ARAB POSITION

2 KRUPPS

VILLAGE WITH
REED HUTS

SHALLOW RAVINE WITH WELLS

SITE OF DERVISH CAMP

= RIFLE PITS
= LOW THIN SCRUB

① 2 KRUPPS, 2 BRASS GUNS,
   1 GATLING GUN
② OPEN ROOFED BRICK
   BUILDINGS
③ IRON BOILER
④ SITE OF DERVISH CAMP

108

The Dervish Attack

Finally, as the square came within 200 yards of the natives, they ceased firing and charged the formation at great speed. The Dervishes seemed impervious to bullet wounds and many fell within five yards of the British lines. The brunt of the attack fell on the Black Watch and the Naval Brigade; hurled back by rifle fire, the natives charged again and again, but not one reached the square, as they were swept away by rifle fire.

On the other side of the square, contact was made and fierce hand to hand fighting ensued, but the Gardner guns of the Naval Brigade came into action and the assault was repelled.

At this point the cavalry swept around the right flank of the square and charged in three lines to their right front where the Dervishes were massed. The cavalry got into difficulties when they were themselves attacked by a large number of Arabs who opened their formation as the initial charge swept by them. Dismounted carbine fire saved the hussars, but not before they had suffered heavy casualties.

The square re-adjusted its ranks and advance was resumed, now pushing through thick, dense bush to reveal many trenches and rifle pits, each containing three or four natives, who fell before the relentless advance.

The square formation was abandoned, the flank formations deployed and the advance continued in two long lines. The infantry encountered stiff opposition, as the Dervishes contested every yard of ground, but supported by artillery, began to clear the rebels from their entrenched positions in the village of El Teb and its wells. By 2pm the action was over, the village and its wells were carried and the natives were seen fleeing towards Tokar and Suakin. General Graham's men lost five officers and 24 other ranks killed, 17 officers and 142 other ranks wounded, while it was eventually estimated that the rebels suffered 2,300 casualties out of an estimated force of 6,000.

The square at El-Teb 29th February 1884.

The Two Sides

We are fortunate in having a fairly complete order of battle for General Graham's command. This has been listed below with the quoted historical strength have been converted into three different figure to man ratios to assist the re-creation of the British force. It is entirely up to the war gamer as to whether or not the support elements and transport animals are represented, but they have been included. It has been assumed that the Hussars serving as mule handlers were additional to, and not deducted from, the 'fighting' strength of the two Hussar regiments.

Some unused Dervish cavalry figures could be pressed into service to represent the Abyssinian scouts, but they took no part in the action, so again, they could be omitted if the war gamer so wishes.

Major General Graham's Force, El Teb 29th February 1884				
	Actual	1:33	1:50	1:100
1st Brigade (Major General Redvers Buller)				
- 1/The Gordon Highlanders	751	23	15	8
- 3/The King's Royal Rifle Corps	610	18	12	6
- 2/Princess Victoria's (Royal Irish Fusiliers)	334	10	6	3
- 6/1 Scottish Division RA (7pdrs)	150	5	3	2
2nd Brigade (Major General Davis)				
- 1/The Black Watch (Royal Highland Regiment)	761	23	15	8
- 1/The York and Lancaster Regiment	400	12	8	4
- Royal Marine Light Infantry	478	14	9	5
- Naval Brigade (Gatling/Gardner guns)	162	5	3	2
- M Battery I Brigade RA (7 and 9pdrs)	126	4	2	1
Cavalry Brigade (Brigadier General Stewart)				
- 10th Hussars	328	10	6	3
- 19th Hussars	410	12	8	4
- Mounted Infantry	126	4	2	1
- Abyssinian mounted scouts	100	3	2	1
26th Field Company RE	**100**	**3**	**2**	**1**
- Various supporting details	200	6	2	2
- Camels	600	18	12	6
- Mules	350	11	7	4
- Ambulance camels	100	3	2	1

Note: As the Arabs were unreliable, dismounted Hussars were used as handlers for the mules carrying ammunition.

There was a total of 20 artillery pieces and six machine guns with General Graham's force. Ratios not withstanding, one model of either a field gun or a machine gun could be included in the British force to represent this element.

Osman Digna's Command

We have far less information with which to analyse the Dervish force at El Teb. The consulted sources do not even agree on the overall strength, with estimates ranging from 10,000 to 12,000.

After due consideration, the lower figure of 10,000 has been selected on the grounds of economy and space - both for figure storage and required playing area.

Recalling that the Mahdi divided his main army into three main sections or 'Flags', it may be safe to assume that the Dervishes at El Teb were all one 'Flag' under Osman Digna.

The natives within the Flags were divided into units of between 800-1,200 men. These in turn were further divided into three fighting formations; the first unit was composed of spearmen, sub-divided into 'standards' made up of tribes or sections of tribes, then came the riflemen and a cavalry unit.

So, armed with this information we can progress and our 'Flag' could be conveniently sub-divided into 10 units of 1,000 each. Each of these units was then further divided into three warrior types - spearmen, riflemen and cavalry. Employing the percentages suggested by the overall Dervish deployment in the Sudan, each 1,000 warriors might be composed of 320 infantry (swords or rifles), 610 spearmen and 60 mounted men.

Once again three figure/man ratios have been suggested, but inevitably the Dervish force is going to require substantial numbers.

Osman Digna's Force, El Teb 29th February 1884

	Actual	1:33	1:50	1:100
Each unit of 1,000	1,000	30	20	10
Spearmen	610	18	12	6
Swords and rifles	320	10	6	3
Mounted	60	2	1	-

Army (assuming 10 of the above units)

	Actual	1:33	1:50	1:100
Spearmen	6,100	185	122	61
Swords and rifles	3,200	97	64	32
Mounted	600	18	12	6
Totals: Approx.	**10,000**	**300**	**198**	**99**

So, to re-create Osman Digna's force at El Teb, the war gamer will need either 300 warriors at the 1:33 ratio, nearly 200 at 1:50 and virtually 100 at the 1:100 ratio.

Bear in mind that this is a purely theoretical figure and those with access to more accurate information on the Dervish army might well wish to vary both its overall strength and the internal composition.

The Dervishes had a couple of Krupp artillery pieces in position on the southern end of the ridge and a further four artillery pieces and a Gatling gun in the village. These were all manned by pressed ganged gunners, but they did open fire on the approaching British, so the war gamer may want to include a token field gun for the Dervishes and not worry too much about the resultant distortion to the figure ratio.

Terrain

For the first part of the action, the British open square was moving over rough terrain of sandy soil and low, thin scrub. Once the square was re-formed after the initial

Dervish onslaught and the advance was resumed, the troops had to push through thick, dense bush, revealing many trenches and rifle pits, each containing three or four natives.

The Dervishes occupied shallow earthworks on a ridge, which must be a major terrain feature. For the pilot games, non-contoured, stepped terrain pieces were used and these worked very well, bearing in mind that initially it is necessary to position the bulk of the Dervishes on the ridge.

Behind the ridge was a shallow ravine containing the wells; these can be represented if required, but this is not essential. The village of El Teb was sited on two hills - one three or four times the size of the other - on the other side of the ravine behind the ridge. The village consisted mainly of reed huts, with a few 'unroofed' brick houses and a fortified sugar refinery plus an iron boiler which belonged to a refinery.

The hills were again represented by stepped or contoured terrain pieces, the larger of the two around two feet long and a foot wide, with a piece about 12 inches square used stand for the smaller hill.

The brick houses and the refinery can be 'standard' Arab type houses which are fairly easy to scratch build or purchase commercially. The boiler is an interesting item, I used a part from a WW2 oil refinery that was in the 'no longer used, but looks useful' box of scenery etc.

The reed huts were represented by hemispherical plastic shapes - originally the packaging for sweets of some sort - painted a straw colour with suggestions of shading, dirt and a doorway being added.

The brick buildings were fortified and defended by the Dervishes, but the reed huts should have no defensive value.

Mechanics

The British marched in square; the leading face consisted of the York and Lancaster Regiment, supported by the Royal Marine Light Infantry. The Gordon Highlanders (right) and the Black Watch (left) made up the flanks, with the King's Royal Rifle Corps and the Royal Irish Fusiliers in the rear. The artillery was in the centre of the square with the cavalry on the right flank of the formation. Although the square lost cohesion at one point, the war gamer should move the British in this formation. The square was assailed on all sides by the tribesmen who knew no fear, falling in droves under the close range massed rifle fire.

After the initial contact the Dervishes withdrew steadily and in good order to prepared positions in and around the sugar refinery and the village. The British advance was resumed and the troops had to push through thick, dense bush, revealing many trenches and rifle pits, each containing three or four natives. This aspect could be represented by allocating perhaps half effect to British firing at the natives occupying such positions. Alternatively, the positions could be allowed 'hidden fire' until the British close within a specified distance, at which point the Dervish positions are revealed. This is not trench warfare; as soon as the enemy approached the tribesmen leapt out of the trench or fire pit and either charged towards their attackers or fell back to new positions.

The Action at Abu Kru 19th January 1885
(The Desert Column of the Gordon Relief Expedition)

An Outline of the Action

For the second action on the war games table, we now turn to a much smaller affair.

On 30th December 1884 Brigadier General Sir Herbert Stewart led his 1,600 strong Desert Column on the first leg of his journey across 150 miles of desert to Metemmeh. The first objective was the wells at Jakdul, some 90 miles south east of the British camp at Korti. The wells were reached on 12th January and, after leaving a detachment to guard them, Stewart moved on towards Abu Klea, the wells there offering the next supply of water. Moving in such a formation was slow work, with frequent stops in order to maintain the cohesion of the square, all carried out in searing heat. The Dervishes attacked the Column at Abu Klea on 17th January and were defeated in a fiercely fought action

After spending the night at Abu Klea, Brigadier Stewart left a small garrison and began to march on to Metemmeh on the banks of the Nile and some 25 miles distant.

After a days uninterrupted progress, a large force of tribesmen was observed between the column and their destination.

The Brigadier halted his men and allowed them a meal before starting work on the construction of a temporary zareba to protect the animals and stores. Unfortunately as his men sat down to eat they came under sniping fire and General Stewart himself was mortally wounded.

Command of the Desert Column passed to Colonel Sir Charles Wilson KCMG RE, an intelligence officer and deputy adjutant general of the relief expedition. Leaving half the Heavy Camel Regiment, the 19th Hussars, the Naval Brigade and the Royal Artillery to guard the hastily constructed camp, Colonel Wilson moved the rest of his command in the customary square formation towards the Nile, intending to establish an entrenched position on the river's bank.

The Dervish Attack

Progress was slow and the Dervishes could be seen on a ridge leading the villages of Abu Kru and Gubat. As his men approached the ridge, Colonel Wilson soon came under attack from tribesmen forming a semi-circle as they swept towards the square at high speed.

Some mounted Arabs seemed to have moved towards the zareba, but this attack didn't amount to much. The two main initial assaults were directed at the left flank and front of the square, to be met with withering fire that caused heavy casualties. More attacks followed, but these were equally unsuccessful and after several assaults had been halted, the Dervishes gave up and melted away.

The British lost one officer and 22 other ranks killed, eight officers and 90 other ranks wounded in the engagement.

The Two Sides

We are again fortunate in having a fairly complete order of battle for Brigadier Stewart/ Colonel Wilson's command. As with the narrative for El Teb this has been listed below with the quoted historical strength have been converted into three different figure to man ratios to assist the re-creation of the British force. One point

Dervish reinforcements arrive.

that should be noted is that all the British troops were mounted on camels, which certainly provides the colonial flavour. Fear not though, as the infantry in square were dismounted during the action, so ordinary infantry figures will fit the bill.

The Desert Column at Abu Kru

Commanding: Colonel Sir Charles Wilson KCMG RE

	Actual	1:33	1:50	1:100
Heavy Camel Regiment (half)	200	6	4	2
Guards Camel Regiment	350	11	7	3
Mounted Infantry Camel Regiment	357	11	7	3
1/The Royal Sussex Regiment	417	13	8	4
Totals:	**1,324**	**41**	**26**	**12**

The Dervishes

Once again, there is far less information with which to analyse the Dervish force at Abu Kru. References are vague about numbers, but there were about 11,000 at the battle of Abu Klea, suffering over 1,000 casualties, so we might venture to organise the Dervishes in the same way as for El Teb.

Suggested Dervish Strength at Abu Kru

Army (assuming 10,000 strong)

	Actual	1:33	1:50	1:100
Spearmen	6,100	185	122	61
Swords and rifles	3,200	97	64	32
Mounted	600	18	12	6
Totals: Approx.	**10,000**	**300**	**198**	**99**

So, once again the war gamer will need either 300 warriors at the 1:33 ratio, nearly 200 at the 1:50 and virtually 100 at the 1:100 ratio to fight at Abu Kru.

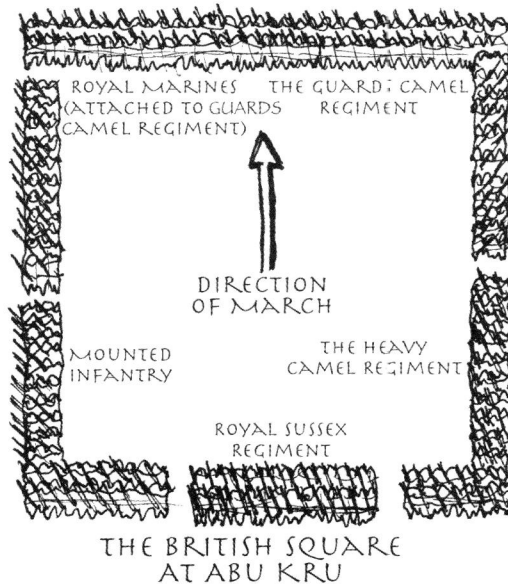

THE BRITISH SQUARE
AT ABU KRU

PLAN OF THE BATTLE
OF ABU KRU
19th January 1885

MOUNTED MEN

GARDNER
19TH HUSSARS
ZARIBA
R.A.

ROYAL MARINES
MOUNTED INFANTRY
GUARDS
SUSSEX REGIMENT
HEAVY CAMEL REGIMENT (HALF)
TO ABU KRU

The square at Abu Kru 19th January 1885.

Terrain

The square seems to have received the Dervish attacks while occupying some raised ground, probably not too elevated and with extended, gentle slopes. The British zareba need not be represented on the table top, although the supporting artillery from the guns in the zareba can be brought into the game.

There is a low, extended ridge to the left of the square and this was initially occupied by the Dervishes, so it would need to be represented on the table top.

Apart from these features, a sandy dry soil, interspersed with the occasional thorn bush will suffice to set the scene.

Mechanics

The British square would have formed up using their kneeling camels as a makeshift defence. It is unlikely that the war gamer has access to over 40 models of kneeling camels - but if they are available, great! - so a compromise will have to be made. Rocks, lichen, boxes, sacks can be pressed into service to give the impression of a light defensive perimeter. If necessary, this can be omitted completely.

Other than that, this scenario is based on firepower against an overwhelming number of spears.

117

In Closing

I sincerely hope that this book has achieved its purpose in encouraging the reader to consider the possibilities of re-creating two important Victorian colonial campaigns.

Suggested Reading

Some of the works to which I have referred when working on this book are listed below. The list is not exhaustive, nor does it include heavy going material; these are readily obtainable, if elderly - books, written by people who know their stuff.

If I could recommend just the one overall work to read for information on the two campaigns, it would be the excellent *War on the Nile* by Michael Barthorp, which also includes an account of The Nile Campaign 1882.

Barthorp, Michael	*British Cavalry Uniforms Since 1660*	Blandford 1984
Barthorp, Michael	*British Infantry Uniforms Since 1660*	Blandford 1982
Barthorp, Michael	*The British Army on Campaign 1816-1902 (4): 1882-1902*	Osprey 1988
Barthorp, Michael	*War on the Nile: Britain, Egypt and the Sudan 1882-1898*	Blandford 1984
Carman, William	*Richard Simkin's Uniforms of the British Army*	Webb & Bower 1985
Chappell, Mike	*British Cavalry Equipments 1800-1914*	Osprey 2002
Chappell, Mike	*British Infantry Equipments 1808-1908*	Osprey 1980
Featherstone, Donald	*Colonial Small Wars 1837 - 1901*	David & Charles 1973
Featherstone, Donald	*Khartoum 1885*	Osprey 1993
Featherstone, Donald	*Omdurman 1898*	Osprey 1993
Featherstone, Donald	*Weapons and Equipment of the Victorian Soldier*	Blandford 1978
Featherstone, Donald	*Victoria's Enemies*	Blandford 1989
Fosten, Don & Marrion, Bob	*The Camel Corps and the Gordon Relief Expedition*	Military Modelling October 1976 - June 1977
Herbert, Edwin	*Handbook for Colonial Wargamers*	Victorian Military Society 1976
Knight, Ian	*Queen Victoria's Enemies (2) Northern Africa*	Osprey 1989
Wilkinson-Latham, Robert	*The Sudan Campaigns 1881-1898*	Osprey 1976

The Internet

As is the way of the world these days, the internet also provided a varying number of sources of varying usefulness, depending on how one words the 'search' request. The information is out there, it just takes some finding sometimes.

One website which is - in my personal opinion - head and shoulders above the rest is Major General Tremorden Rederring's Colonial-era Wargames Page (http://zeitcom.com/majgen). This relates and illustrates (in colour) fictional conflicts in a place called Ouargistan, set in the late 19th and/or early 20th century. In addition to the battle/war game reports, there are pictures of war game figures, buildings, scenery, various types of ships and boats and so on. There are details on how to construct a war game model of a native dhow. The site was created by four war gaming friends in Texas and does not seem to have been updated since 2004, but there is a wealth of inspiration and information there.

The Victorian Military Society

The Victorian Military Society is an international society whose principal aim is to encourage and foster the study of military aspects of the Victorian era. The dates of study are extended to include the period between the end of Queen Victoria's reign and the beginning of The Great War in 1914.

The Bengal Lancers at Hasheen 20th March 1885.

The Society publishes a quarterly journal *Soldiers of the Queen*, each issue contains a number of articles on diverse topics, accompanied by maps, illustrations and photographs - all members of the Society are encouraged to submit articles for publication.

The Soldiers Small Book is the Society's newsletter and contains information and news for members.

Within the Victorian Military Society are a number of Special Interest Groups, voluntary associations of Society members who wish to take an interest in a particular aspect of Victorian military affairs. At the time of writing (2007) these Groups include Anglo-Boer Wars; First and Second Anglo-Boer Wars, India Burma; Armies and wars of the HEIC, Britain and India, Sudan Wars; Sudan Campaigns of 1883-1908, The Diehard Company; living history with the 57th Foot (Middlesex Regiment); Wargames; award winning war gamers, Zulu War: Anglo-Zulu Wars and Zulu history, Internet Group; an internet list/message service for VMS members only.

The Victorian Military Society also holds an annual military fair.

If you are interested in joining the Society, the current (2007) annual subscriptions are UK £17, Europe £20, Worldwide (surface mail) £20, Worldwide (air mail) £25. Due to the high cost of processing foreign currencies, subscriptions are requested in cash, cheque, credit or standing order. Please post with your payment or credit card details with your address to The Honorary Publicity Officer, The Victorian Military Society, PO Box 58377, Newbury, Berkshire RG14 7FJ, United Kingdom.

The Society has a web page www.vms.org.uk which will provide more information.

The Heliograph

The Heliograph magazine is dedicated to 'historical miniatures gaming of the colonial variety' and is published six times a year. The contact point is Richard Brooks, 207 Ivory Key Road, Saluda, South Carolina 29138 USA. Subscriptions (2006) are $18 USA, £21 Canada and £15 for European customers. Subscribers in Australia and New Zealand should contact Castaway Arts for further details. Other overseas subscribers are asked to contact Richard Brooks. The magazine has a website www.theheliograph.com and subscriptions can be taken on line.

Savage and Soldier

Savage and Soldier, one of the classic publications for colonial war gamers is available once again. The magazine will complement *The Heliograph* by focusing more on historical articles, just like it did 'in the old days'

Savage and Soldier is published four times a year. Charter subscriptions are $21 USA, $25 Canada, £15 for European customers. After the charter subscription time has expired, the rates are $25 USA, $30 Canada and £18 for Europe. The contact point is Richard Brooks, 207 Ivory Key Road, Saluda, South Carolina 29138 USA. Subscribers in Australia and New Zealand should contact Castaway Arts.

Combined Subscription

The Heliograph website offers the opportunity to subscribe to both The Heliograph and *Savage and Soldier* at the same time. The rates are $36 USA, $50 Canada, £30 for Europe. The contact point is Richard Brooks, 207 Ivory Key Road, Saluda, South Carolina 29138 USA.

Back Issues

All back issues of *The Heliograph* and *Savage and Soldier* are handled by Robert W Burke Jr, 1919 Mount Conness Way, Antioch, California 94531 USA.

The Continental Wars Society

As its name indicates, The Continental Wars Society concentrates primarily on European conflicts, generally set in the post-Napoleonic, pre-Great War period. Apart from the Society's quarterly periodical *The Foreign Correspondent* being an excellent read and full of hard-to-find information, some of articles do occasionally feature colonial conflicts and I thoroughly recommend the publication. Examples of colonial subjects that have appeared include The French capture of Algiers 1830, The March to Timbukto, The French in Dahomey in the 19th century and the Dutch East Indies Army. The current (2006) UK annual subscription in £6. Cheques should be made out to, and sent to, Ralph Weaver, 37 Yeading Avenue, Harrow, Middlesex HA2 9RL.